Praise for *Amplify AI*

MW00838127

Walking down a busy New Yc̲ ̲ ̲ ̲ ̲,̲ ̲ ̲ ̲ ̲ ̲ ̲ ̲ explained in the deepest and most sincere way—how he's advocating for AI ethics and humanity, and in the same breath shared the most brilliant and effective ways to leverage AI. Over the sounds of taxi horns and street performers, his voice carried a compelling narrative, one I was later able to read in this book. It was then that I realised the depth of his passion and expertise and how it will shape the future of AI, identity, and business. His deep care for our identities is only rivalled by his deep knowledge, and practical applications to help us all uplevel and learn.

JASMINE STAR, speaker, podcaster and CEO of Social Curator

Amplify AI is the guide to your AI business strategy. We're talking human smarts, AI firepower, and age-old wisdom all working together. It's not about replacing your team with robots; it's about creating a future where tech and humanity work in perfect harmony.

DAN MARTELL, *Wall Street Journal* bestselling author of *Buy Back Your Time*

How you use AI is everything! Ronsley not only has the knowledge he is sharing in his book, *Amplify AI*, but he also the best guide to important ethics around the power use of these tools. This book cuts through it all so you can use AI for good and for the expansion of your output.

DARIN OLIEN, *New York Times* bestselling author, Emmy-winning producer and co-host of *Down to Earth with Zac Efron* on Netflix

From the big picture ethical complexities, down to tactical prompts to help you build a better business, this book has it all.

GLEN CARLSON, co-founder of Dent.Global

Ronsley's *Amplify AI* is a game-changer. This book breaks down complex AI strategies into actionable steps, making it accessible and ethical for any business. With a focus on real-world applications and maintaining core values, Ronsley provides a comprehensive guide to integrating AI in a way that enhances efficiency and drives sustainable growth. It's the perfect playbook for leaders committed to smart, responsible innovation and ensuring their business thrives in the digital age.

ROB ANGEL, creator of Pictionary and author of *Game Changer*

You know that when Ronsley Vaz steps in, it's a sign of the future unfolding. The great news is you can throw away that foggy crystal ball because *Amplify AI* shows you, clearly and practically, how to leverage this disruption to create the business of your dreams.

LEANNE HUGHES, author of *The 2-Hour Workshop Blueprint* and host of the *First Time Facilitator* podcast

Ronsley Vaz is one of the world's top minds when it comes to smart utilization of AI, and his practical knowledge will save you hundreds of hours while maximizing your productivity and giving you precious time back. If you're ready for some crazy AI shortcuts and some massive time savings, then Ronsley is your man.

BEN GREENFIELD, *New York Times* bestselling author of *Boundless* and founder, Ben Greenfield Fitness

Amplify AI will teach you how to ethically integrate AI into your business, balancing cutting-edge technology with our core human values. Reading this book is a smart move for any forward-thinking leader.

TRIVINIA BARBER, founder, Known Partners

Amplify AI is a no-BS guide to making AI work for your business without losing your soul. This playbook is loaded with actionable strategies and a clear-cut plan to turn AI from a buzzword into your business's secret weapon, and real-world tactics to streamline your operations, skyrocket productivity, and drive serious growth. If you're ready to harness AI the right way, without any compromise, this is your go-to resource.

TAKI MOORE, founder, Million Dollar Coach and author of *Million Dollar Coach*

Amplify AI is the roadmap to understanding and successfully implementing AI in your business. Ronsley Vaz has done an exceptional job collecting and curating what you need to know, and then deleting everything you don't. If you want a rock-solid guide to AI for business, this is it.

DALE BEAUMONT, founder and CEO, Business Blueprint

Amplify AI positions AI as a strategic partner rather than a replacement, framing technology as an enabler of human advancement rather than a threat. It offers a comprehensive strategy for fully leveraging AI's capabilities, while upholding a human-centric approach in business.

YURI ELKAIM, *New York Times* bestselling author, health expert and founder, Healthpreneur

Amplify AI champions a mindful approach to technology, providing actionable strategies to harness AI in ways that uphold human values. Discover how AI can boost performance while reducing mental load and preserving the essence of human creativity.

DR SHERRY WALLING, founder of ZenFounder, bestselling author, speaker, and podcaster

Amplify AI masterfully bridges human intelligence and AI, providing business leaders with a practical, ethical roadmap for integration. Ronsley Vaz inspires readers to embrace AI as a powerful ally, enhancing decision making and innovation. This book is an essential guide for navigating the future of intelligent business transformation.

NEIL SAHOTA, IBM Master Inventor and author of *Own the A.I. Revolution*

Want to simplify your understanding of AI? Read Ronsley's new book: *Amplify AI*—a practical guide to the ethical use of artificial intelligence in business. As he has done so successfully in the podcast space several years back, Ronsley jumps to the front of the line on AI, going deep in his immersion and understanding, allowing the cream to rise to the top for the reader's consumption.

JAMES ORSINI, President of Startup Operations, VaynerX

Everyone is exclaiming "AI is the future" and "you need to start using AI in your business today," but no one is telling you how...until now. In his new book *Amplify AI*, Ronsley Vaz details not only how to use AI successfully, but also how to use it with strong ethics and a clear conscience. Grounded in concepts from indigenous wisdom, empathy, and the science of earning trust, you will receive a holistic approach to incorporating AI into your business operations. You'll also be able to do it more successfully (and responsibly) than you ever thought possible.

JOEY COLEMAN, international keynote speaker and WSJ bestselling author of *Never Lose an Employee Again*

Amplify AI is a refreshing and invaluable read. Ronsley Vaz doesn't just rehash the basics of AI; he dives deep into the nuances of integrating AI ethically and effectively across all aspects of business. His *Amplify AI* Pyramid and SymbioEthical framework offer a structured approach that even seasoned AI users will find enlightening. What really resonated with me was Vaz's emphasis on the symbiosis between human intelligence and AI. He articulates beautifully what many of us in the field have experienced: that AI isn't about replacement, but enhancement of human capabilities. The book is filled with insights that challenged me to think differently about how I approach AI strategy. Whether you're just starting out or have been working with AI for years, *Amplify AI* offers fresh perspectives and practical strategies that can take your business to the next level. It's a must-read for anyone serious about leveraging AI to its full potential while staying true to their values.

AMY YAMADA, speaker, business coach, and founder, IdealClient.ai

Meeting Ronsley in Dubai was a turning point. As he passionately shared his groundbreaking AI work, I saw a man who didn't yet realise the world-changing impact he was creating. On the drive back to his hotel, I simply told him: "Thank you for your work." I'll never forget the shock in his eyes—he hadn't fully grasped the profound power of what he was building. *Amplify AI* is one part of this power— unleashed. This book is the blueprint for turning AI into your greatest ally. It will help you build what was once unimaginable, transform your business, and leave others wondering how you did it. Read it, apply it, and soon, someone will thank you for your work, too.

LEOPOLD AJAMI, public speaking and ethical persuasion coach and founder, Novel Philosophy Academy

In business, speed is everything, right? *Amplify AI* helps you accelerate your game with no-nonsense frameworks and AI tricks you can use today to get ahead. This book isn't about barely surviving this technological shift—it's your roadmap to adapting, thriving and operating in the future while others are still figuring out the present.

IGOR POGANY, founder, *The AI Advantage* YouTube channel and community

Amidst an overwhelming explosion of content on AI technologies, *Amplify AI* stands out and is the one book I'm recommending to everyone. This book doesn't just talk about AI; it offers a comprehensive strategy for leveraging AI to gain a competitive edge, whether for yourself or your team. Ronsley Vaz has crafted a toolkit that equips you to delegate the robotic tasks to AI, freeing up your time and energy for higher-level thinking and creativity. Vaz's Amplify AI is a masterclass in how to integrate AI ethically and effectively into your business. His ability to weave enduring concepts that will remain relevant as the field of AI evolves is particularly noteworthy. I'm confident that this book will become a landmark in the AI landscape.

JERE L SIMPSON, CEO, Atlas UP, AI innovator and productivity revolutionist

If you want to understand sustainable business growth and success, think in terms of innovation, amplification, and Ronsley Vaz's *Amplify AI*. This book is the blueprint for ethical AI integration that propels true business transformation in ways never before imagined.

KISMA ORBOVICH, founder and CEO of Illumination Academy™ and Prosperity Code™ coaching method

RONSLEY SERIOJO VAZ

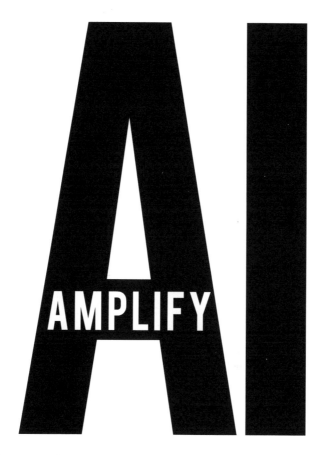

AI AMPLIFY

Integrating Intelligence, Preserving Humanity
—a Guide for Business Acceleration

GRAMMAR
FACTORY
— EST⁰ 2013 —

Published by Grammar Factory Publishing, an imprint of
MacMillan Company Limited.

Grammar Factory Publishing
MacMillan Company Limited
25 Telegram Mews, 39th Floor, Suite 3906
Toronto, Ontario, Canada
M5V 3Z1

www.grammarfactory.com

Vaz, Ronsley.
Amplify AI: Integrating Intelligence, Preserving Humanity—
a Guide for Business Acceleration / Ronsley Vaz.

Paperback ISBN 978-1-998756-83-4
Hardcover ISBN 978-1-998756-85-8
eBook ISBN 978-1-998756-84-1

1. COM004000 COMPUTERS / Artificial Intelligence / General.
2. BUS025000 BUSINESS & ECONOMICS / Entrepreneurship.
3. COM079000 COMPUTERS / Social Aspects.

PRODUCTION CREDITS
Cover design by Designerbility
Interior layout design by Setareh Ashrafologhalai
Book production and editorial services by Grammar Factory Publishing

GRAMMAR FACTORY'S CARBON NEUTRAL PUBLISHING COMMITMENT
Grammar Factory Publishing is proud to be neutralising the carbon
footprint of all printed copies of its authors' books printed by or
ordered directly through Grammar Factory or its affiliated companies
through the purchase of Gold Standard-Certified International Offsets.

CONTENTS

INTRODUCTION

M Y WIFE, ROCHELLE, and I don't agree on who said 'I Love You' to the other person first. I sincerely believe she said it first. She just outright refutes that fact. We carry two different versions of history and don't know which one is true. That is how bad human memory is.

What if we didn't have to read or remember all the relevant data needed to make great decisions and solve meaningful problems on the planet? What if we could augment our shortcomings—our poor memory, long processing times, and our need for extensive brain energy—with a silicon-based intelligence? A silicon-based intelligence that has a large memory, quick processing times, and is now easily available, for free, on the internet.

When we believe someone has a high IQ, it means that that person has a high working memory. You now have access to just such a high IQ. Intelligence that can ace all known human-grading exams. And you just need a computer, internet, and know-how to access it.

Don't get me wrong—this book isn't just about adopting new tech; it's about embracing a future where AI is your ally, enhancing every aspect of your business from operations to customer engagement, all while staying true to your core values.

Have you ever felt overwhelmed by the volume of information you need to process each day? Or wished you could clone yourself to tackle that ever-growing to-do list? As humans, we face inherent limitations on how much we can remember, how quickly we can learn, and how accurately we can execute. But what if there was a way to augment our abilities, to transcend these limitations and unlock new possibilities?

Throughout history, we've witnessed how transformative technologies have propelled us forward. The printing press, electricity, the internet—each of these innovations reshaped society, expanded our capabilities, and fundamentally altered the way we live and work. AI is poised to be the next great leap, and its potential impact goes farther than we can see.

Imagine a world where you have instant access to all the information you need, analysed and synthesised to guide your decisions. Picture a workday where routine tasks are handled with machine-like efficiency, allowing you to focus on innovation and strategic thinking. Imagine a future where your products and services are tailored to the unique needs of each customer, fostering deep loyalty and growth. This is the promise of AI—to augment our intelligence, overcome our limitations, and unlock a future where businesses can achieve what was once deemed impossible.

Think of this book as the spider that bit Peter Parker. When you're done with this book, you will feel superhuman and will be able to do what you once thought was impossible.

I promise.

What Do I Know?

You might be thinking, 'Okay, Ronsley, what makes you the guy to guide me through this AI revolution?' Well, let me tell you, I've been obsessed with the power of technology since I was a kid pulling computers apart in my bedroom.

That curiosity led me to a Bachelor's in Computer Science and Engineering, a Master's in Software Engineering, and then, because understanding people is just as important as understanding code, an MBA focused on Psychology and Leadership.

All that education aside, my passion has always been helping people raise their voices and share their stories. That's why I dived headfirst into the world of podcasting eleven years ago. Since then, I've created podcasts for some of the most well-known figures on the planet—actors, athletes, politicians, entrepreneurs, healers. My podcasts have been downloaded over 5.1 million times across 133 countries. I even had the honour of giving a TED Talk on the power of deep conversations.

Through my award-winning podcast agency, We Are Podcast, I've helped countless businesses and individuals amplify their message and connect with their audience. But as the digital landscape has shifted, I've seen a new way of doing things emerge. And I'm not talking here about just automating tasks; this is about unlocking human potential and global intelligence on an entirely new level.

That's why I founded Amplify AI, a training and advisory company that helps businesses adopt AI ethically and effectively. In contrast to chasing the latest tech trends, we're focused on building a future where AI empowers people to achieve what was once unimaginable.

The data backs this up. Corporate investments in AI exploded from $17 billion in 2013 to over $276 billion in 2021.[1] The demand for AI skills is skyrocketing, with AI-related job postings increasing over 350% in recent years.[2] It's clear that AI is more than a buzzword; it's a force reshaping the world as we know it.

This book is the culmination of my decades-long fascination with technology, my passion for empowering voices, and my deep commitment to ethical business practices. I'm an AI geek, I'm not denying it! But more than that, I'm an entrepreneur who's walked the walk, using AI to transform my own businesses and those of my clients. I've seen first-hand the incredible power of AI when it's aligned with human values and a clear vision for the future.

There's need for a new narrative around AI that moves beyond fear and competition towards collaboration and mutual benefit. I want you, the world's business leaders, to adopt a more humanistic and ethical approach to AI adoption.

AI as Your Ally

You start by gathering data, the lifeblood of AI, in a way that feels like listening to the stories your customers and operations tell. This isn't about numbers and charts; it's about understanding the narrative behind the data.

Next, you dive into making sense of this information. It's like decoding a secret message that guides your business decisions, aligning them with your brand's identity and values.

Then, you streamline operations, not by replacing humans with robots, but by freeing up your team to focus on what they do best—innovating and connecting with customers.

After this, you customise your AI solutions, which isn't a one-size-fits-all affair. Here you are tailoring technology to fit your business like a glove, enhancing your brand's unique voice and mission.

Predictive insights come next, offering a crystal ball into future trends, enabling you to seize opportunities before they even knock on your door.

Leading the market through innovation is the cherry on top. You set the pace, rather than struggling to keep up. You look at forming partnerships and exploring new territories with the confidence of a trailblazer, all while ensuring your ethical compass guides you every step of the way.

Through this book we're focusing on growth, ethics, and human-centric innovation. We're creating a legacy that reflects the best of what it means to be a leader in the digital age—a leader who's driven, compassionate, and forward-thinking.

So, as you turn each page, remember, this affects more than the future of your business; you're shaping the future of how businesses operate in harmony with technology and humanity. I challenge you to think of AI not as a tool but as a teacher, a mentor who can prompt us to be more human, more compassionate, and more innovative. Together, let's embrace this idea of making AI something beyond a tool in our arsenal—making it a partner in our quest for a brighter, more connected world.

Integrating AI in 3 Parts

This book is presented in three parts. In Part 1, we are going to deepen our understanding of the barriers to and benefits of AI adoption, looking at the role of visionary leadership in this space and examining the mistakes we need to avoid and the stages we'll go through in the process.

Part 2 presents a framework for integrating AI into your business in an ethical, sustainable, and symbiotic way that aligns with your business goals. It is a marriage between five parameters that I call the SymbioEthical Framework.

Part 3 of the book is going to guide you through a framework for integrating AI into your business, which is embedded in a model I call the Amplify AI Pyramid. This provides a strategic roadmap for organisations to integrate Artificial Intelligence ethically and responsibly, in alignment with their brand identity and business objectives.

The framework consists of six steps:

1. Identify

This initial step focuses on clearly defining the organisation's core identity, values, vision, and goals to establish a strong foundation for AI adoption. Taking the time to conduct internal reviews and align stakeholders sets the stage for AI initiatives that are purpose-driven and that support strategic priorities.

2. Interpret

In this analytical stage, leveraging data and AI itself can offer valuable insights into the motivations and behaviours of target audiences and illuminate operational strengths and pain points. A thorough interpretation grounded in facts ensures AI integration will be customised for and relevant to the organisation.

3. Streamline

Once current processes are well understood, this optimisation stage focuses on using AI automation and augmentation to increase efficiency, productivity, and experience. The priority is refining and enhancing standard workflows before pursuing AI integration.

4. Customise

With core operations and audiences clarified, AI personalisation comes into play to tailor and refine interactions, engagement strategies, and sales approaches. Done ethically, customisation promotes stronger connections.

5. Predict

Transitioning the organisation from reactive to proactive, this anticipatory stage harnesses AI predictive capabilities for data-driven forecasting. This guides partnerships, market strategies, and workforce planning.

6. Amplify

The final step concentrates on sustainably expanding the AI integration to amplify the organisation's reach, trust, impact, profitability, and legacy. The focus is responsible scaling aligned with ethics and brand values.

This sequence allows a strategic, ethical, and brand-aligned rollout of AI across the enterprise. We start with a strong identity-focused foundation before optimising, customising, predicting, and finally amplifying results with integrated AI that enhances operations, interactions, and innovation.

Let's see the results this generates.

Major Business Outcomes

All businesses are looking to flourish and, with that, they are looking for four major outcomes: growth in revenue, growth in audience, growth in brand, and growth in operations. These outcomes enable the business to create profit, impact, trust, and legacy.

Grow Revenue

Growing revenue is vital for sustainability and scaling. Without revenue growth, businesses risk stagnation and lose competitive edge. The common mistake made when businesses are trying to grow revenue is an overemphasis on short-term gains over long-term strategy.

Imagine your business as a tree. Just as a tree relies on its roots to absorb nutrients for growth, your business needs revenue to thrive and expand. Growing revenue is similar to ensuring the tree has ample water, sunlight, and nutrients. Without this growth, the tree becomes stagnant, wilting in the competitive forest of the market.

Now, the common mistake here is focusing solely on the leaves (short-term gains) and neglecting the roots (long-term revenue streams). Businesses often chase immediate profits through aggressive sales tactics or short-lived promotions. It's like watering the leaves of the tree but ignoring its roots.

In contrast, sustainable revenue growth involves nurturing relationships with customers, developing a strong value proposition, and innovating products or services to meet evolving market demands.

Consider a local cafe that doesn't only sell coffee, but also creates a community space for art and music. This attracts a broader customer base and opens new revenue streams like event hosting or merchandise sales. This approach of intertwining community needs with business offerings exemplifies nurturing the roots of the tree for long-term revenue growth.

The book ties revenue growth to AI's ability to predict opportunities, customise sales conversations, and amplify profits. This involves identifying and interpreting vital signs relevant to business growth and streamlining product sales.

Grow Brand

Growing the brand of the business builds trust, recognition, and loyalty. A lack of brand growth can lead to obscurity in a crowded market. A mistake made when businesses are growing their brands is neglecting brand consistency and not aligning brand values with audience expectations.

Growing your brand is like crafting a compelling story. A well-narrated story captivates the audience, making them return for more. Similarly, a strong brand resonates with customers, building trust and loyalty. If the story (brand) isn't engaging or gets lost amidst others, it fails to leave an impact, much like a book that remains untouched on a shelf.

A common mistake in brand growth is inconsistency— similar to a storyteller who changes the plot midway. This confuses the audience (our customers) and dilutes the brand message. It's essential to maintain consistent brand voice, aesthetics, and values across all channels. An example is Patagonia, a company that has successfully grown its brand by consistently promoting environmental sustainability, thus attracting customers who share similar values.

Another aspect to consider is aligning the brand with customer expectations. Imagine a tech company that prides itself on innovation but has an outdated website. This misalignment can deter potential customers.

AI can play a role in brand growth through predicting partnerships, customising brand templates, and amplifying trust. It can assist in establishing brand identity and interpreting brand guidelines.

Grow Audience

Growing the audience that is exposed to your business's brand is essential for expanding market reach and influence. Without audience growth, businesses fail to capitalise on new opportunities. A common mistake businesses make when growing their audience is focusing only on acquisition, while neglecting audience engagement and retention. I wrote about the different types of audiences that exist in my first book, *Amplify*, and described how there are Listeners, Leads, Prospects, Clients, Advocates, and Partners.

Growing an audience is like planting a diverse garden. You need various plants (audience segments) to make the garden (market presence) vibrant and appealing. Without a growing audience, your garden remains small and unnoticeable, limiting its appeal.

The mistake here often lies in focusing only on planting new seeds (acquiring new customers) while neglecting the nurturing of existing plants (engaging and retaining the current audience). It's important to water and tend to the plants you already have, ensuring they grow and flourish.

A business that uses personalised email marketing to keep in touch with existing customers, offering them relevant content and products, is effectively nurturing its garden. Compare this to a business that only offers incentives to new clients.

Understanding the unique needs and preferences of different audience segments is like knowing the right conditions for different plants. A business that recognises and caters to these diverse needs can grow a robust and loyal audience.

Audience growth is gained through AI's ability to predict new markets, customise audience engagement, and amplify impact. This involves interpreting an audience's 'WHY' stack and streamlining audience attention.

Grow Operations

Scaling operations improves efficiency and productivity. Stagnant operations, on the other hand, can lead to increased costs and reduced agility.

Improving operations is like tuning a machine to work at optimum efficiency. If operations don't grow and evolve, the machine starts to rust and lag, reducing productivity and increasing costs.

A common pitfall in this arena is resisting change, particularly technological advancements. Think about the time wasted using an old map in the age of GPS. Businesses that fail to adopt new technologies and processes risk falling behind. Take cloud-based solutions as an example. This can streamline data management and improve collaboration, similar to upgrading from a manual assembly line to an automated one.

It's important to focus on optimising existing processes. It's not just about adding new gears to the machine, but also ensuring the existing ones are well-oiled and functioning seamlessly. Regularly reviewing and refining operational processes can lead to significant improvements in efficiency and productivity.

Operations growth can be achieved via AI's capability to predict cognitive load reduction, customise AI solutions, and amplify legacy. AI's contribution includes identifying business methods and interpreting operational blocks.

These four growth areas, like individual cogs in a larger machine, work together to drive the business forward. Understanding and nurturing each aspect is crucial for the holistic growth and success of the enterprise.

How to Use this Book

Starting this process of integrating AI into your business can feel like there are new options to consider every week. Whether you're a solopreneur, a boss running a bustling small business, a director steering a medium-sized enterprise, or a CEO commanding a large corporation, the principles of *Amplify AI* offer a compass to guide you through this maze.

For the Solopreneur

Imagine you're a craftsman, your business a canvas where every stroke counts. AI is your palette, offering endless colours to bring your vision to life. Use AI to automate the mundane, freeing you to focus on your craft. Tools that manage your schedule, automate customer interactions, and help with content creation can be extensions of your creative process, amplifying (pun intended) your ability to connect, create, and sell without diluting the personal touch that defines your brand.

AI is creating a huge gap in society. On one side, we have those who are hyper-consuming, fuelled by AI's ability to push them to buy more, watch more, and scroll more. On the other side, we have the hyper-creators, who are using AI to build businesses, generate content, and make a bigger impact in the world.

This is the 'create-consume wedge' that entrepreneur Daniel Priestley warns us about. If you're caught in the consumption trap, it's hard to break free. But if you can embrace AI as a tool for creation, you'll be able to reach your full potential and make a real difference in the world.

> To learn more about this, tune in to episode 62 on the *Amplify AI* podcast: 'The Impact of AI on Entrepreneurship feat. Daniel Priestley'. Find the podcast on Spotify, YouTube, or wherever you listen to your favourite podcasts.

For the Small Business

Running a small business is similar to captaining a ship through uncharted waters. AI can serve as both your compass and your lookout, helping you navigate and spot opportunities on the horizon. Implement AI to streamline operations, from inventory management to personalised customer experiences. Let AI analyse the vast ocean of data to uncover insights about your customers, and empower you to tailor your offerings and plot a course to new markets with confidence.

AI enables you to delegate. It can take on those repetitive tasks, freeing you to focus on strategy, innovation, and building relationships. It's a powerful way to accelerate your growth and achieve more in less time.

When you have a strong framework for your business, AI can take that framework to the next level. AI can help you generate content, create pitches, and even personalise your offerings based on your established processes, enhancing your existing systems and strategies.

For the Medium Business

As a medium business, you're a bridge between the nimble startup and the established corporation, embodying the best of both worlds. AI is your tool to scale personalisation and efficiency, turning data into actionable insights. Use AI to deepen your understanding of customer needs, automate personalised marketing at scale, and enhance the decision-making process. It's about maintaining the agility of a small business while laying the groundwork for the infrastructure and innovation that drive growth.

For the Large Enterprise

In large enterprises, AI can be a strategic partner in innovation and sustainability, enabling you not only to lead in your industry but redefine it. Invest in AI to explore new business models, enhance customer experiences, and drive operational efficiencies. But remember, with great power comes great responsibility; I can't emphasise enough the importance of ethical AI use, transparent governance, and mitigation of biases. Your leadership in responsible AI adoption can set a standard, inspiring others and leaving a legacy that transcends profit.

In every case, using AI doesn't aim to replace the human element. We're amplifying it. We're augmenting our capabilities, enabling us to solve meaningful problems and connect more deeply with our audience.

Amplify AI is your playbook to do this thoughtfully, ethically, and effectively, ensuring that as you integrate AI into your business, you do so in a way that honours your unique identity and the values you hold dear.

This book is a call to action, an invitation to join a transformation that goes beyond mere technological adoption. Envision a future where AI and humanity collaborate, creating a synergy that amplifies the best of what both can offer. Leverage AI not just as a tool for growth, but as a catalyst for positive change and innovation, and leave a legacy that resonates with your audience and the wider world.

> To self-diagnose where your business can get the most out of adopting AI, complete the Amplify AI Scorecard, which you can find at amplifyais.com.

PART 1

ADOPTING AI

CHAPTER 1

CONSCIOUSNESS—
IN BETWEEN
REASON AND LOVE

Visionary leaders see beyond the immediate fog of uncertainty. They envision a future where positive AI contribution isn't a distant shore but a tangible reality, woven into the fabric of their business.

IF NOTHING ELSE, my hope is that this book allows you to challenge your current opinions and ideas. By all means keep to your current ways of doing things, but only after you've opened your mind to consider other perspectives. It is important to understand that the same event can be seen differently depending on a person's underlying belief system and the frequency of an event's occurrence.

There was a time when most people didn't think intelligence and information were important. And the ones who realised the opposite then harnessed them to take things that didn't belong to them. This is why access to information was the first privilege taken away from slaves. That and their ability to use their voice.

Educating yourself with information is key to intelligence. It also helps with perspective. The more diverse information we have access to, the better informed our perspective, and a well-informed perspective improves empathy, which raises consciousness. When we do academic research, we have to look at all the different perspectives in our literature review before we present our thesis and the method we are going to use to prove or disprove our thesis. Perspective is everything. A lack of perspective is ignorance.

We humans need to get to a higher state of consciousness. And this starts with each of us—each of us raising our own consciousness.

Mapping Consciousness

Dr David Hawkins' book *Power vs Force* presents a fascinating exploration of human consciousness and its impact on personal and global development. Hawkins introduces the concept of a 'Map of Consciousness', which assigns numerical values, ranging from 0 to 1,000, to different emotional states, reflecting their energetic vibration and impact on an individual's life.

1   **Lower Vibrational Frequencies**: These are associated with feelings of shame (20), guilt (30), apathy (50), grief (75), and fear (100). Individuals operating at these frequencies often experience life as challenging, with a sense of victimhood and powerlessness.

2   **Mid-Range Frequencies**: These include desire (125), anger (150), and pride (175). While these emotions are energetically higher than the lower vibrations, they are still characterised by ego-driven motivations and can lead to conflict and suffering.

3 **Transformation Point**: Courage (200) is a pivotal point in Hawkins' scale. At this frequency, individuals start to empower themselves, shifting from negative, life-suppressing energies to positive, life-affirming ones.

4 **Higher Vibrational Frequencies**: This range includes neutrality (250), willingness (310), acceptance (350), and reason (400). These states are marked by increased emotional stability, openness, and intellectual growth.

5 **States of Love and Beyond**: Love (500) is a significant leap in consciousness, characterised by a sense of unconditional love and wellbeing. Joy (540), peace (600), and enlightenment (700–1,000) are the highest states, where individuals experience profound harmony, interconnectedness, and spiritual transcendence.

Hawkins believes that by elevating our consciousness and vibrational frequency, we improve our personal lives and positively influence the collective human experience. His work suggests that even a small number of individuals operating at higher frequencies can counterbalance the negativity generated by those at lower frequencies, leading to transformative global effects.

Depending on what frequency you are at, you can see the same event differently. A leader who is operating from a place of fear will see things very differently from someone operating from a place of willingness or peace.

Tune into a deep conversation I had with Kylie Ryan on the *Amplify AI* podcast, episode 83, about this. We talk about how fear, blame, and mistrust can create adversarial relationships, while collaboration and understanding foster positive outcomes. This is even more important for AI.

Now, AI isn't just a tool for automating tasks. It's a new form of intelligence that has the potential to change the way we think, interact, and even understand ourselves. This is a conversation we're just starting, and it's going to be a big one.

Remember, however, that AI is only as good as the data it's trained on. And when AI makes mistakes, it's called a hallucination. Think of it like this: if you ask ChatGPT for legal precedents, it might just make them up. That's because it doesn't understand the nuances of legal research. It's trying to provide the best match based on what it knows, but it might not be able to discern what's real and what's not in this context. We need to be mindful of these limitations and provide AI with the right data and prompts to ensure it's generating accurate and useful information. If we do that, its potential is unlimited.

> In episode 64 of the *Amplify AI* podcast, my conversation with Neil Sahota, a leading AI expert, really brought home the profound impact of AI. Neil mentioned that AI is essentially this version of intelligence that's just coming into focus. It's like the big bang of intelligence. And the potential for AI to change the world is huge, much bigger than we can imagine. It's going to be a wild ride, and I think it's important to be prepared.

Why Ethical AI Adoption Is up to Leaders and Businesses

With great power comes greater responsibility. If we've been blessed to lead, whether in life, in business, or at the badminton club on Fridays, I consider that a blessing. Leaders wield a lot of influence. Influence over thoughts, behaviour, and actions.

We are also the changemakers.

The Role of Visionary Leadership

Think of visionary leaders as ship captains navigating the uncharted waters of AI. They aren't just steering the vessel; they're charting a course towards a horizon brimming with potential. Just as a captain must understand the sea, leaders must grasp the vast ocean of AI—its currents, depths, and the treasures it holds beneath.

Visionary leaders see beyond the immediate fog of uncertainty. They envision a future where positive AI contribution isn't a distant shore but a tangible reality, woven into the fabric of their business. They understand that AI isn't just about algorithms and data; it's about unlocking new possibilities, very similar to discovering new lands. These leaders are not just adopters but pioneers, setting a precedent for others to follow.

However, this journey requires more than vision. It demands courage—the courage to embrace change, to invest in novel technologies, and to lead teams into new territories. Like a skilled captain who knows when to sail or when to wait out the storm, visionary leaders balance risk with opportunity, ensuring their ship is always sailing towards progress.

Ethical Leadership and AI

With AI, ethical leadership is an imperative, rather than a choice. As leaders, we wield the power to shape AI, to mould it in a way that reflects the values and principles of the business and the leaders who make decisions for the business. It's like being handed a piece of clay; what we create from it can be either a testament to our ethical standards or a misshapen representation of overlooked responsibilities.

As leaders, we need to appreciate that this is the time of 'the creative'. In the age of AI, creativity emerges as a paramount human quality that technology seeks to augment, not replace. This celebrates the creative potential unleashed by AI, freeing humans from repetitive tasks to engage in higher level, creative endeavours. It highlights the collaborative future where human ingenuity is amplified by AI capabilities, fostering an environment where innovation flourishes. Leaders can encourage others to leverage AI in ways that elevate creative pursuits, emphasising the unique contributions of human creativity in this AI-enhanced world.

Ethical use of AI is like walking a tightrope. On one side, there's the potential to revolutionise how we operate and interact; on the other, there's the risk of infringing on privacy, perpetuating biases, and causing unintended harm. Ethical leaders walk this tightrope with precision and care, ensuring that every step taken with AI is measured, considered, and aligned with the greater good.

Such leaders use AI to optimise operations or enhance profitability while also employing it to uplift, transform, and innovate responsibly. They set the bar high for data privacy, actively work to eliminate biases in AI algorithms, and maintain transparency in their AI endeavours. In doing so, they become leading businesses who are leading a movement towards a more ethical and equitable AI-driven future.

Championing Collaboration

When it comes to AI integration, collaboration is the thread that binds different parts of the organisation together. Leaders who champion collaboration understand that AI isn't a one-department show. Each department plays a critical part, and it is what they create together that leads to success.

Fostering a collaborative environment is like hosting a grand feast where every guest brings a unique dish to the table. Each department—from IT and Operations to Marketing and HR—brings its expertise, insights, and perspectives.

Together, they create a meal far richer and more diverse than anyone could have prepared alone.

Leaders must encourage this meeting of minds, breaking down silos and fostering a culture where ideas and knowledge flow freely. They must create spaces—both physical and digital—where conversations spark, partnerships form, and innovation thrives. In doing so, they maximise the benefits of AI and cultivate a workplace where collaboration is the norm, not the exception.

Communicating the AI Vision

Communicating the AI vision means sharing a picture so vivid, so compelling, that everyone from the boardroom to the front lines can see their part in it. It's a responsibility that every member of the team bears together.

A leader's role in this is crucial. We must articulate not just the what and the how of AI, but the why. Why is AI important to business? How does it align with the organisation's goals and values? How will it impact each team member, and what does it mean for their future?

But this isn't a one-time announcement; it's an ongoing dialogue. As the use of AI evolves, so must the conversation. As leaders, we must keep the lines of communication open, updating the team on progress, addressing concerns, and celebrating milestones. This ongoing dialogue ensures that the AI vision remains clear, relevant, and inspiring for everyone involved.

I know, I know, it sounds a bit out there—talking about AI as a living thing. But bear with me. What if this silicon-based intelligence isn't just lines of code? What if it's an emerging life form, a digital brain mirroring our own, with a capacity to learn, adapt, and even create? Think about Tesla's self-driving cars—those machines aren't just following instructions; they're processing data, making decisions, and evolving their 'driving style' in real time. They have memories, just like us. They make mistakes, like us. And just like us, the data they consume shapes their worldview. AI is alive, and it's time we start treating it as such.

Hopefully, I've painted you a picture of what a positive future could look like—and how our leaders can get us there. So what's holding people back?

CHAPTER 2

THE BARRIERS
TO ADOPTING AI

*The democratisation of AI—ensuring it's access-
ible and understandable to all—is paramount
if we want to use its potential for good.*

THE OPPORTUNITY IS here, but navigating the path of
AI adoption is not without its challenges. Though the
destination is worth the effort, the process can be rough.
Here are some of the barriers we face when considering
integrating AI into our business.

Cost Concerns

The cost of AI can be scary, especially when some of the
'experts' are throwing around big numbers! And the price of
any associated software isn't as big a concern as the spend
on training required for your people to adopt it.

This is like considering a major upgrade to your business's infrastructure—the initial cost can be high (though it
doesn't always have to be), but the long-term benefits often

outweigh these initial expenses. Sections of this book will cover the ROI of AI and offer scalable, cost-effective AI solutions that can help mitigate these concerns.

In episode 85 of the *Amplify AI* podcast, I discuss the lengthy process of a manual SWOT analysis and OKR process taking between 4 and 11 weeks, depending on the complexity and size of the business. Listen to this episode to understand the costs of not using AI to do a lot of business tasks.

Lack of Expertise

Entering the AI world without a map or a guide can leave leaders feeling lost. Especially with a lot of online coaches calling themselves AI experts to get the attention of leaders looking for solutions. Many companies just don't have the right people on their team to handle AI.

I hear this sentence a lot: 'ChatGPT can't do simple maths.' Yes, asking ChatGPT to do maths is like throwing your clothes at a vacuum cleaner and expecting it to run a wash cycle. This is a sign of ignorance. Use a calculator for maths. Or write some code that will perform maths functions.

This issue is similar to knowing you need to reach a destination, but not knowing the best path or the right people to help you get your business there. This leads businesses to waste time, effort, and energy trying different AI tools suggested by people just learning AI for the first time. Investing in training and considering partnerships with AI experts can be effective strategies.

Uncertainty about ROI

AI, for many, is still a leap into the unknown. Especially if you don't know how machine learning and deep learning algorithms work. Using ChatGPT makes everything look easy, but does it really offer a return on investment and grow the business?

I hear CEOs ask all the time, 'Will AI actually help my business?' This uncertainty makes them hesitate to take the first step on a potentially rewarding process. Starting off small and demonstrating clear use cases and success stories can help identify the tangible benefits of AI. Imagine all the employees of your business competently using intelligence to reduce their cognitive load, freeing them up to be more creative. That is unquantifiable ROI in my opinion.

> In episode 87 of *Amplify AI*, I use Claude.ai to estimate between 6 and 12 weeks for streamlining product sales without AI, along with potential cost breakdowns. This dialogue showcases the time and cost benefits of AI adoption when done correctly.

Data Challenges

AI is only as good as the data it learns from. Amassing incomplete or biased data sets is like trying to finish a puzzle with missing pieces—the picture will never be complete. Just like we humans need food and water to survive, AI needs data and power to work.

The cleaner the food we eat, the more productive and healthier we are. The cleaner and more diverse the data AI has, the better it can perform. You really need to make sure your data is good. Think of it like food for AI—the better the data, the better the results!

Cultural Resistance

Change is often met with resistance. This especially comes from leaders who feel like they need to know it all. I've heard leaders tell me how competent they are with AI, only for me to realise a few minutes later that they have just been playing with ChatGPT for a while. It's like when everyone with a Facebook account was a social media expert. What we find is that people who haven't taken the time to understand AI's true capabilities are the ones who are swift to oppose the idea of changing things up to integrate it into operations.

Bringing in AI can be like trying to change the flow of a river—you're going to get some resistance! Building a culture that embraces change, values the reduction of human cognitive load, and prioritises continuous learning is vital.

Let's be honest—the fear of AI taking our jobs is real. And it's not just some Luddite paranoia. My friend and fellow entrepreneur Cameron Herold put it bluntly in episode 73 of the *Amplify AI* podcast: 'The only employees who should be worried about losing their jobs to AI are those who don't actually leverage and use AI day to day.' It's like refusing to use the internet in today's business world. Sure, you might survive for a while, but you're setting yourself up for irrelevance. AI is the new electricity. Embrace it, learn to use it, or risk being left in the dark.

Ethical and Privacy Concerns

When it comes to business and AI, ethical considerations and privacy issues are usually the last thing on leaders' minds. But missteps can be costly. Imagine using AI without considering the ethical implications of this new technology. Once your brand trust is affected, it is very hard to rebuild.

Even AI pioneers struggle with its ethical complexities. Take Elon Musk, for instance. Remember when he publicly went head-to-head with OpenAI—the very company he co-founded? He accused them of straying from their initial mission to 'benefit humanity' and instead prioritising profits for Microsoft, their major investor. This high-profile clash highlights a critical question: How 'open' is OpenAI really?

While they argue that closed systems prevent misuse of powerful AI, critics counter that this lack of transparency hinders independent audits and the development of safeguards.

> Tune in to episode 85 of the *Amplify AI* podcast to hear me talk through this issue in detail.

It's a delicate tightrope walk, balancing innovation with responsibility. The democratisation of AI—ensuring it's accessible and understandable to all—is paramount if we want to use its potential for good. After all, we don't want AI to become a tool wielded only by a select few, potentially amplifying existing power imbalances.

Addressing these concerns head-on, with transparent policies and ethical AI practices, is essential. The Symbio-Ethical Framework in Part 2 of this book will help sort these issues out.

Integration Complexities

Seamlessly integrating AI into existing systems can be as complex as composing a symphony. Each element of the orchestra must be harmonious. As a software engineer who has written a thesis on software quality and taken two companies to an ISO9001 accreditation, I know that nailing the processes in your business is everything. Using your current processes and adopting AI to make them more efficient and effective is the best way to simplify its adoption.

Customisable and adaptable AI solutions, designed to fit into the unique ecosystems of different businesses, can ease this integration process. And there are many reasons to engage with them.

Speaking of these, let's look at some of the benefits.

CHAPTER 3

THE BENEFITS AND STAGES OF ADOPTING AI

*Instead of solely amplifying existing strengths,
leaders should also focus on how AI can
mitigate weaknesses within our organisations.*

USED TO SAY, and I still do, 'The best thing about a podcast is that it's easy to do. The worst thing about a podcast is that it's easy to do.' The exact same principle applies to adopting AI. Using ChatGPT is easy, but does that mean it's helping your business?

I've come to realise a lot of us are not big fans of Artificial Intelligence. But let's start by refusing to be the intelligent beings that fear intelligence. Embracing AI as a different form of intelligence is essential in today's rapidly evolving business space. We're talking about unlocking the true potential of your business by merging the human spirit with the inhuman capabilities of Artificial Intelligence. This means we need to start seeing AI as an ally, not an enemy! Fear often stems from the unknown; thus, demystifying AI and understanding its capabilities and limitations is key.

This way of thinking encourages leaders to adopt a mindset of curiosity and openness, leveraging AI to enhance decision making, creativity, and problem solving. By embracing AI, businesses can uncover new opportunities, streamline operations, and deliver exceptional value, ensuring that we remain at the forefront of our industries.

We need to change how we see AI, and use it with *empathy and love*. This way, we can harness AI not just as a tool for efficiency but as a means to genuinely solve problems and positively impact lives. Leaders can prioritise empathy and love in their AI strategies, ensuring that the technology is applied in ways that enhance human dignity and wellbeing.

The Advantages of Adopting AI Using the Amplify AI Pyramid

Before we head into the stages you'll go through when adopting AI, I want to highlight what I see as the three specific benefits to your business of integrating it using the methods outlined in this book:

1. Strategic AI Alignment

Imagine a ship heading out to sea with no clue where it's going. This is like implementing AI in business without strategic alignment. AI, like a powerful engine, needs a direction, and a purpose aligned with the core goals of the business. Without this, AI becomes a tool without a cause, potentially leading to wasted resources and misaligned efforts.

Now, consider the transformative power when AI and business strategy are in perfect harmony. AI's capabilities, from data analysis to automation, are directed towards specific, strategic goals. This alignment ensures that every aspect of AI integration—whether it's customer service enhancements, process automation, or data-driven decision making—directly contributes to the overarching objectives of the business.

When executed correctly, the results are unmistakable: enhanced efficiency, increased competitive edge, and a clear ROI from AI investments. Businesses become technology-empowered, steering towards their defined destination with more precision and speed.

2. Operational Efficiency

Neglecting operational efficiency in AI integration is like trying to run a marathon without training—you might make some progress, but it's unsustainable and inefficient. In today's dynamic business world, operational efficiency isn't just nice to have; it's a necessity for survival and growth. AI, when not aligned with improving operational processes, can lead to chaos, underutilisation, or even pointless effort.

However, when AI is leveraged correctly, it becomes a catalyst for streamlining operations. From automating mundane tasks to optimising complex workflows, AI can transform the operational landscape of a business. This efficiency means not only doing things faster, but also doing them smarter, reducing errors, saving costs, and freeing up human talent for more creative and strategic endeavours.

The impact of this is profound. Businesses experience a significant boost in productivity, a smoother flow of operations, and an overall uplift in employee morale and customer satisfaction. Operational efficiency becomes a competitive advantage, setting the stage for scalability and innovation.

3. Predictive Insights

Disregarding the predictive capabilities of AI is like sailing a boat while ignoring the weather forecast—you're at the mercy of unforeseen circumstances. In the volatile seas of the business world, predictive insights are crucial for navigating challenges and capitalising on opportunities. Without this foresight, businesses risk being reactive, always a step behind in a fast-paced market.

Embracing AI for its predictive power, however, can transform a business's approach from reactive to proactive. By analysing trends, customer behaviours, and market dynamics, AI provides invaluable foresight. This ability to predict enhances decision making and prepares businesses for future challenges and opportunities.

The results are tangible. Businesses that use predictive insights are better positioned to anticipate market shifts, understand customer needs, and innovate ahead of competitors. This foresight leads to more-informed strategies, targeted investments, and ultimately a stronger, more resilient business ready to lead into the future.

I'm hoping I've convinced you! You're going to see this all work out for your business step by step, so next let's take a look at the stages you'll go through.

The Stages of Adopting AI

When you begin adopting AI in your business, it is the technological implementation that leads to transformation, impact, and expansion. Each stage of AI adoption is a significant pit stop on this adoption curve.

1. Awareness
This is where curiosity is piqued. Everyone is curious about AI at the minute. Business leaders, much like listeners tuning into the first episode of a new podcast, begin to understand the potential of AI.

Here, the focus is on education and exploration, like dipping your toes in the ocean of AI possibilities. It's about understanding the basics: What is AI? How can it benefit your business? This stage is super important—it will prepare you for everything that happens next.

2. Exploration

Now, the business starts experimenting, much like a chef trying out new ingredients. This stage involves pilot projects and initial integrations, where AI is tested in controlled environments.

What tends to happen in this stage is businesses copy and paste prompts to see what is possible. They witness intelligence. The key here is to learn from these experiments, understanding what works and what doesn't, refining the recipe until it's just right. At this stage, remember that serving even the best dish to an audience that doesn't like certain ingredients is wasting the effort put into preparing the dish. Use AI specifically for your business and the goals the business is trying to achieve.

3. Early Adoption

This stage involves implementing AI solutions in specific areas of the business.

Start where your business is struggling the most. If you aren't good at creating content marketing, start here. If your business needs standard operating procedures to streamline operations, that is where you begin. It's about taking calculated risks, learning from successes and failures, and beginning to see tangible benefits. It's the stage where the theoretical becomes practical, and AI starts to show its true value.

4. Maturity

Here, AI is no longer a novel concept but an integral part of the business fabric. The business is a well-oiled machine, with AI seamlessly integrated into various business processes. Efforts at this stage are about optimisation and refinement, and continuously improving and adapting to new challenges and opportunities.

This is where you can track and predict the reduction of your teams' cognitive load, and identify new products and markets. Businesses here have not just adopted AI; they have embraced it as a core part of their strategy. This is where you amplify the impact of AI on your business's revenue, operations, audience, and credibility.

I get asked all the time, 'Where do I start, Ronsley?' Well, start with your shortcomings. Leveraging AI to address our shortcomings is a humble yet strategic approach to technology integration. Instead of solely amplifying existing strengths, leaders should also focus on how AI can mitigate weaknesses within our organisations. This approach encourages a culture of continuous improvement and adaptability.

So it's clear where to start and it's clear where we're headed. Before we get into the nitty gritty, though, I want to warn you what mistakes to watch out for.

CHAPTER 4

MISTAKES TO AVOID WHEN ADOPTING AI

AI has a ton of potential, just like a tiny
seed that can grow into a huge tree.
But you need to plan for that growth.

THROUGHOUT THE ADOPTION process, there are seven common mistakes companies make when adopting and using Artificial Intelligence. Beware the issues listed here:

1. Misalignment between AI and Business Strategy

This is a mistake I've made, and I bet many other business leaders have too. It is when AI becomes a shiny new toy that businesses want to play with, rather than a tool strategically chosen to meet specific business objectives.

Let me tell you, I've been there, done that, and got the t-shirt when it comes to misaligning AI with business strategy. A few years ago, I got so excited about this AI tool that promised to revolutionise my podcast production process that I jumped in headfirst without really thinking through how it fitted into my overall goals. Big mistake. It was like trying to fit a square peg into a round hole. The tool itself was great, but it wasn't the right solution for my business at that time. Lesson learnt—always start with your strategy and then find the AI tools that align with it.

Often, in the excitement of adopting new tech, or due to pressure to keep up with the AI Joneses, businesses rush AI integration without anchoring it to their strategic plan. A tell-tale sign is when the discussion around AI is more about the technology itself than how it serves the business goals.

Envision AI as a member of your team who needs a clear role that serves the business's vision, not just a passerby doing tricks for applause. Start with your business goals and reverse engineer to find the AI solutions that best drive these objectives. It's about the destination, over and above the ride.

2. Misidentifying Problems and Solutions

On a related note, would you use a map of Paris to navigate the streets of Tokyo? You might have a superb map, but if it's not for the right city, it won't help you reach your destination.

Don't just grab the first AI tool you see! Make sure it's actually going to solve your problem.

Shift your perspective to match the tool to the task, not the task to the tool. As with goals, clearly define the problem you're trying to solve and seek out AI solutions designed to address that specific issue rather than following pointless tools in the wrong direction.

3. Compromising Data Quality and Impact

Garbage in, garbage out—it's an old computing adage that rings particularly true with AI. If you feed your AI subpar data, it's like nourishing your body with junk food; the results are predictably lacklustre.

This slip-up occurs in the rush to get AI up and running without taking the time to cleanse and prepare the data fuelling it. Look for inconsistent data sources, a lack of data governance, or the absence of a data-cleansing process.

Treat your data like a gourmet meal for AI. The quality of the ingredients can ruin or enhance the dish. Invest in robust data management practices. To train AI models effectively, ensure the data is high-quality, relevant, and diverse.

4. Neglecting Data Bias

Talking about diversity, imagine only listening to opinions from a small group of friends—it might feel affirming, but it's hardly a balanced view.

Data bias results when collecting or selecting data for AI without considering how representative and inclusive that data is. We end up with data sets that don't reflect the diversity of the real-world scenarios the AI will encounter.

See your data as a tapestry that should reflect the rich diversity of the world it's meant to serve. Actively seek out diverse data sources and regularly audit AI systems for biases, correcting them as needed.

If we feed AI biased data, we're going to get biased results. Imagine an AI system trained on a dataset that predominantly features male CEOs. Guess who it's going to recommend for leadership positions? The issue is that much of the data we've captured throughout history reflects existing inequalities. It's on us to ensure the data we use to train AI is diverse, representative, and free from harmful biases.

Tune in to listen to me talk about this in detail in episode 73 of the *Amplify AI* podcast.

5. Inadequate AI Testing

Would you launch a ship without thoroughly testing it in all types of weather? Sure, it might sail fine on a sunny day, but how will it fare in a storm?

In the eagerness to deploy AI solutions, businesses often cut corners on comprehensive testing. We see rushed AI deployments or limited testing scenarios that don't reflect the complexities of real-life applications.

Think of testing AI like trying out a new recipe before serving it to your guests. Commit to rigorous, extensive testing of AI models across diverse scenarios to ensure robustness and reliability before full-scale deployment.

6. Overlooking Long-term AI Planning

This is like planting a tree but not planning for its growth. Without room to grow, the tree's roots will become constrained, and its potential stunted.

During the initial stages of excitement about AI's immediate benefits, considering its future evolution within the business is often neglected. There is no clear roadmap for scaling AI solutions or integrating future AI advancements.

AI has a ton of potential, just like a tiny seed that can grow into a huge tree. But you need to plan for that growth. So develop a scalable AI strategy that anticipates future business needs, data evolution, and technological advancements.

7. Ignoring Ethical and Legal Concerns

Are you one of those people who skips the terms and conditions when installing new software? It might seem fine now, but it could lead to serious consequences down the line.

When the pressure to innovate overshadows the due diligence required to ensure AI's ethical and legal compliance, it results in a lack of conversations about the ethical implications of AI use and its impact on brand reputation.

Consider AI ethics not as a hurdle, but as a foundational pillar that supports the integrity and longevity of your brand. Embed ethical considerations into the AI lifecycle, from design to deployment, ensuring compliance with legal standards and societal values.

The idea behind highlighting these common mistakes is to let you know what to avoid from the start. Now that we've done that, we can take a look at the big picture—and that last point—in more detail. How can we manage the integration of AI in an ethical way?

PART 2

THE ETHICAL USE OF AI

CHAPTER 5

THE FOUNDATIONS FOR ETHICAL CONSIDERATIONS

Ethical considerations are insanely important, especially when AI systems are making decisions that directly impact people's lives.

WHEN IT COMES to Artificial Intelligence, considering how to adopt and use AI with the best intentions to gain the best results is key.

To start from a brand-new way of thinking about ethics is a waste of energy and effort. There are three main areas that already exist where we can gain clues that can guide our ethical use of AI: previous studies, indigenous wisdom, and algorithms found in nature.

Academia and Entrepreneurship

I'm a certified engineer. I was accredited by the Institute of Electrical and Electronics Engineers, or IEEE—that's the gold standard for engineers. In fact, I was accredited twice.

First when I completed my Bachelor's degree in Computer Science and Engineering before coming to Australia, and second when I completed my Master's in Software Engineering at Griffith University in Brisbane. IEEE is the gold standard for the frameworks and systems to be followed, so trust me when I say the studies here are robust and very well checked.

IEEE Global Initiative on Ethics of Autonomous and Intelligent Systems

The IEEE Global Initiative on Ethics of Autonomous and Intelligent Systems has formulated a set of seven general, ethically aligned design recommendations, which aim to guide engineers and developers in creating AI systems that are both technically robust and ethically sound. These are like guidelines to build AI that's actually good for everyone.

The design recommendations run as follows:

1 Human Wellbeing, Health, and Flourishing
2 Beneficence
3 Autonomy
4 Justice
5 Non-Maleficence
6 Respect for Privacy
7 Accountability

The first principle, 'Human Wellbeing, Health, and Flourishing', emphasises the importance of designing AI systems that prioritise human wellbeing and happiness over mere efficiency or productivity gains. This can be compared to a city planner designing public spaces that serve as functional transportation hubs and also promote relaxation, community engagement, and overall happiness for the city's residents.

The second principle, 'Beneficence', encourages AI developers to create systems that are designed to benefit all stakeholders involved, without causing harm or disadvantage to any group. This concept can be likened to a chef preparing a meal that caters to the diverse dietary preferences and requirements of their guests, ensuring that everyone enjoys their food while feeling included and respected.

The remaining five principles focus on aspects such as transparency, accountability, privacy, fairness, and non-maleficence in AI design. In essence, these recommendations serve as a set of guiding principles to ensure that AI systems are built with ethical considerations at their core.

Ethical considerations are insanely important, especially when AI systems are making decisions that directly impact people's lives. Imagine a lending company developing an AI-powered system to evaluate loan applications. The system seems efficient, but it has been trained on historical data that unfortunately reflects existing biases in the financial system. The result? The AI starts unfairly denying loans to people from certain demographics, perpetuating inequality rather than promoting fairness. This scenario highlights the crucial 'Justice' principle within the IEEE guidelines, emphasising that AI systems must be designed and deployed with a deep commitment to fairness and non-discrimination.

Transparency is another cornerstone of ethical AI. Let's consider a hospital that's using an AI system to help doctors diagnose medical conditions. To build trust with patients, the hospital implements a system that provides the AI's diagnosis and also clearly explains the factors that contributed to that decision. This approach aligns with the 'Transparency' and 'Accountability' principles within the IEEE guidelines, ensuring that the AI's decision-making process is understandable and accountable to both patients and medical professionals.

We must also consider data privacy as a core ethical consideration. Think about a social media platform that uses AI to personalise content recommendations. While this might seem harmless on the surface, imagine if the platform starts collecting and utilising user data without their explicit consent. This scenario raises serious privacy concerns and directly relates to the 'Respect for Privacy' principle outlined by the IEEE. It underscores that businesses must prioritise data privacy and user control over personal information, ensuring that AI is not used to exploit or manipulate users.

The study 'Innovative Business Models Driven by AI Technologies: A Review' explores the symbiotic relationship between AI advancements and business innovation, aiming to uncover how AI reshapes business landscapes.[3] It analyses AI's role in enhancing operational efficiency, driving data-informed strategies, and fostering customer-centric practices. Through comprehensive analysis, the paper presents a blueprint for integrating AI ethically and effectively, underlining the necessity for businesses to adapt and innovate responsibly in the face of AI's disruptive potential.

The findings reveal an understanding of AI's impact, suggesting a strategic approach that balances technological integration with ethical considerations. This equilibrium ensures that businesses leverage AI for competitive advantage and also navigate the associated challenges thoughtfully. The study advocates for a proactive stance in adopting AI, where businesses are encouraged to use its potential while remaining vigilant regarding the ethical and operational intricacies involved, setting a foundation for sustainable growth and innovation in the digital age.

Entrepreneurship Solving Meaningful Problems

There are many businesses that solve meaningful problems for people. And, while I'll give you a few more examples at the end of this section, I want to highlight IBM Watson Health.

IBM Watson Health, launched in 2015, was born out of a vision to revolutionise the healthcare industry through the application of Artificial Intelligence and advanced analytics. The driving force behind this venture was IBM's commitment to leveraging technology to solve complex societal challenges, particularly those related to health and wellbeing.

The problem that IBM Watson Health sought to address was the growing need for more efficient, accurate, and personalised healthcare services. With an ageing global population, escalating healthcare costs, and a rising prevalence of chronic diseases, there was a pressing demand for innovative solutions to improve patient outcomes while also reducing costs.

IBM Watson Health aimed to solve this problem by developing an AI-powered platform that could analyse vast amounts of medical data from various sources (such as electronic health records, clinical trial results, and genomic information) and generate actionable insights for healthcare professionals. These insights included personalised treatment recommendations, predictive analytics for early disease detection, and improved drug discovery processes.

The unique approach adopted by IBM Watson Health can be attributed to its focus on addressing complex societal challenges through the application of AI technology. This aligns well with the concept of Ethical AI Usage in Business:

* **Empathy.** IBM had always been known for its commitment to corporate responsibility. By focusing on using AI technology to solve healthcare problems, the organisation exemplified how businesses can use AI responsibly while still delivering tangible benefits like improved patient outcomes and reduced costs.

* **Transparency.** Another defining aspect of IBM Watson Health's strategy was its focus on being transparent about the data they collected, analysed, and shared with healthcare professionals. This transparency ensured that

all relevant stakeholders were well-informed about how their data was being used and shared, generating valuable insights that could ultimately help improve patient care outcomes.

The vision was that Watson could mine this data to provide insights to improve medical diagnosis, treatment recommendations, drug development, clinical trial matching, and more. IBM partnered with leading institutions like Memorial Sloan Kettering Cancer Center and MD Anderson Cancer Center to develop Watson for applications like oncology.[4]

In the end, however, Watson Health faced many challenges and ultimately failed to meet its ambitious goals.[5] Issues included:

- Difficulty generalising insights from one dataset to new patients
- Inability to understand unstructured data like doctors' notes
- Providing irrelevant or unhelpful treatment recommendations
- Resistance from physicians who didn't want to be told what to do by an AI
- High costs of development and maintenance
- Privacy concerns about patient data
- Regulatory hurdles

After spending over $5 billion and employing 7,000 people at its peak, IBM Watson Health was essentially a failure. In January 2022, IBM sold the data and analytics assets of Watson Health to private equity firm Francisco Partners for just over

$1 billion. The rise and fall of IBM Watson Health provides cautionary lessons about the challenges of applying Artificial Intelligence in the complex healthcare domain, and the gap between hype and reality. Despite the setbacks, many still believe AI and machine learning have great potential to transform medicine if these technologies can be developed and deployed effectively.

Here are five other case studies that could help inform us.

1 **NVIDIA Deep Learning Institute (DLI)**: NVIDIA DLI focuses on educating developers, data scientists, and researchers on AI technologies, best practices, and ethical considerations when implementing AI solutions in various industries. This initiative promotes responsible use of AI by fostering a community of knowledgeable professionals who can make informed decisions about its adoption and implementation.[6]

2 **Prodsmart**: Prodsmart uses AI to optimise manufacturing processes, reduce waste, and increase efficiency. By analysing real-time data from the shop floor, it helps businesses make better decisions regarding inventory management, work orders, and quality control measures. This application of AI in manufacturing demonstrates how responsible use of technology can lead to improved sustainability practices and cost savings.[7]

3 **Unity Technologies**: Unity is a platform for developing interactive 3D content and games using AI algorithms to improve animation, rendering, and character movement. This allows game developers to create more immersive and realistic experiences for players while also saving time and resources in the development process. By focusing on enhancing user experience through responsible

use of AI technology, Unity serves as an example for other businesses looking to integrate AI into their products and services.[8]

4   **Affectiva**: Using AI to analyse facial expressions and emotional reactions, Affectiva helps companies create more-effective advertising campaigns and improve user experiences in products like video games and smart home devices. This application of AI in market research demonstrates how technology can be used ethically and responsibly to gain valuable insights into consumer behaviour without infringing on individual privacy.[9]

5   **SenseTime**: Specialising in computer vision and deep-learning technologies, SenseTime has applied its AI solutions across various industries such as smart cities, autonomous driving, and facial recognition systems. By focusing on addressing ethical concerns related to privacy and data security, SenseTime sets an example for other businesses looking to integrate AI into their operations while staying true to the core principles underlying what it means to be an ethical AI business.[10]

The Asilomar Conference and the 23 Principles for Beneficial AI

The Asilomar Conference on Beneficial AI gathered experts in the field to discuss the ethical implications of this technology and establish guidelines for its responsible use.[11] The result was an agreement on twenty-three principles designed to ensure that AI systems contribute positively to society while minimising potential risks and harms.

These twenty-three principles can be likened to the foundation of a sturdy building, with each principle providing support in a different area of concern. For instance, the

'Respect for autonomy' principle emphasises the importance of AI respecting human decision-making capacity. Meanwhile, the 'Non-discrimination' principle acts as a safeguard against unfair treatment based on attributes such as race or gender.

These principles serve as a comprehensive checklist to help businesses navigate the complex landscape of AI development and deployment. By adhering to these guidelines, companies can use the power of AI to their advantage and also help create a safer, fairer, and more transparent digital world for everyone involved.

The twenty-three principles are grouped into three categories: Research Issues, Ethics and Values, and Longer-Term Issues. Here are the principles:

Research Issues:

1 **Research Goal**: AI research should be focused on beneficial intelligence, not undirected intelligence.

2 **Research Funding**: Investments in AI should be accompanied by funding for research to ensure its beneficial use.

3 **Science-Policy Link**: There should be a constructive and healthy exchange between AI researchers and policymakers.

4 **Research Culture:** A culture of cooperation, trust, and transparency should be fostered among AI researchers.

5 **Race Avoidance:** Teams developing AI systems should actively cooperate to avoid corner-cutting on safety standards.

Ethics and Values:

6 **Safety**: AI systems should be safe and secure throughout their operational lifetime.

7 **Failure Transparency**: If an AI system causes harm, it should be possible to ascertain why.

8 **Judicial Transparency**: AI systems should be subject to equivalent standards of accountability as humans.

9 **Responsibility**: Designers and builders of advanced AI systems are stakeholders in the moral implications of their use.

10 **Value Alignment**: AI systems should be designed so their goals and behaviours align with human values.

11 **Human Values**: AI systems should be designed and operated to be compatible with human dignity, rights, freedoms, and cultural diversity.

12 **Personal Privacy**: Individuals should have the right to access, manage, and control the data they generate.

13 **Liberty and Privacy**: The application of AI to personal data should not unreasonably curtail people's real or perceived liberty.

14 **Shared Benefit**: AI technologies should benefit and empower as many people as possible.

15 **Shared Prosperity**: The economic prosperity created by AI should be shared broadly.

16 **Human Control**: Humans should choose how and whether to delegate decisions to AI systems.

17 **Non-subversion**: AI systems should not be designed to subvert human values.

18 AI **Arms Race**: An arms race in lethal autonomous weapons should be avoided.

Longer-Term Issues:

19 **Capability Caution**: There being no consensus, researchers should avoid presuming that AI has low or high limits on its future capability.

20 **Importance**: Advanced AI could represent profound changes in life on Earth, and should be planned and managed with commensurate care.

21 **Risks**: Risks posed by AI systems, especially catastrophic or existential risks, should be subject to planning and mitigation efforts.

22 **Recursive Self-Improvement**: AI systems designed to recursively self-improve or self-replicate should be subject to strict safety and control measures.

23 **Common Good:** Superintelligence should only be developed in the service of widely shared ethical ideals, and for the benefit of all humanity rather than one state or organisation.

These principles are aimed at guiding the development of AI in a manner that maximises its benefits while minimising potential harms and ethical concerns.

Algorithms in Nature

Nature, through evolution and adaptation, has developed efficient, sustainable, and often complex processes that could be likened to algorithms. Thinking of them like this is a way to understand the inherent systems and patterns that guide the behaviour of flora and fauna, which can serve as inspiration for guiding AI. Here are some examples illustrating this principle.

Bird Migration Patterns

Birds use a set of rules for migration, which can be incredibly precise and efficient. They navigate using Earth's magnetic fields, the position of the sun and stars, and even olfactory cues. This natural 'algorithm' ensures that they travel thousands of miles with minimal energy waste, following the most efficient routes to their destinations.

The precision and efficiency of bird migration patterns are remarkable. In AI, this can inspire algorithms for path-finding and route optimisation, such as in logistics and navigation systems, where efficiency and energy conservation are paramount. For instance, city planners can leverage AI algorithms inspired by bird migration patterns to optimise traffic flow, reduce congestion, and improve fuel efficiency, mimicking the efficient route planning of birds.

> There have been a few studies done on bird migration patterns. In fact, I interviewed an ornithologist called Jean-Phillippe Schepens Van Thiel on the *Amplify AI* podcast. We talked about how we can use these patterns to inform and inspire AI. Tune in to episode 36, 'Nature's Algorithms and AI'.

Diving Deeper into Nature's Code

Before I talk about other algorithms, I would like to highlight three case studies to show how bird migration patterns have optimised applications. Let's start with Boveiri and Elhoseny (2018), who proposed an Adaptive Cuckoo Optimisation Algorithm, inspired by the cuckoo's egg-laying and breeding behaviours (Boveiri and Elhoseny, 2018).[12]

Cuckoo Optimisation Algorithm:

Have you heard of the cuckoo bird? It's a master of deception, and lays its eggs in other birds' nests. This cunning strategy of survival and adaptation in the animal kingdom has inspired the Cuckoo Optimisation Algorithm (COA). Think of it like a computer program that tries to find the best solution to a problem by mimicking how cuckoos find the best nests to lay their eggs. COA is used for solving complex optimisation problems in various fields, from engineering design to resource allocation. It's about finding the most efficient way to do something, just like those clever cuckoos!

Adaptive Cuckoo Optimisation Algorithm:
Now, imagine taking the basic principles of COA and giving it an adaptive twist. That's the Adaptive Cuckoo Optimisation Algorithm (A-COA).[12] It's like teaching an old dog new, smarter tricks. The A-COA tackles the common optimisation problems and does so with a 25.85% improvement in performance compared to the basic COA. It's like finding a faster route than the well-trodden path.

In AI, this means we're looking at a system that's not just efficient but also adaptable—a key trait for tackling the ever-evolving challenges in fields like logistics, engineering, and even in complex decision-making scenarios in business.

Animal Migration Inspired Group Mobility Model:
In 2019, Verma and Kesswani introduced a model based on the migration behaviour of animals like birds and fish called the Animal Migration Inspired Group Mobility (AMIGM) model. This overcomes the limitations of existing mobility models and realistically simulates real-world scenarios (Verma and Kesswani, 2019).[14]

Picture a flock of birds or a school of fish moving in unison, each individual seamlessly aligning with the group. This natural spectacle is the inspiration behind the AMIGM model. Verma and Kesswani observed the limitations in existing mobility models for mobile ad hoc networks (MANETs) and asked, 'What if we mimicked nature?' The result? A more realistic, efficient, and adaptable model for simulating movements in MANETs, much like how a flock of birds optimises its flight pattern.

For AI, this is a leap towards more natural, fluid network dynamics. Imagine drones that adjust their flight patterns like a flock of birds, optimising for energy and coverage. Or consider mobile networks that adapt like swarms, offering robust and efficient connectivity.

Now, let's shift gears to a more sombre yet vital arena—healthcare. Specifically, the battle against prostate cancer, showcasing the application of these natural algorithms in medical data analysis.

In 2020 Prabhakar and Lee saw an opportunity to apply the principles of Migrating Birds Optimisation to classifying prostate cancer—a significant leap from nature to medical data analysis.[15] Their model translates the efficiency of birds migrating across continents into a tool that sifts through medical data, seeking out patterns and answers.

This study is a profound example of AI stepping into a realm where precision and accuracy can have life-altering implications. It opens doors to AI systems that can interpret complex medical data and also aid in early diagnosis and personalised treatment plans.

These examples show us how intelligent birds are and what we can learn from them.

Ant Colony Optimisation

This is a classic example of a natural algorithm. Ants find the shortest path from their colony to a food source using pheromones. This process has inspired computational algorithms for solving complex optimisation problems by mimicking the pheromone trail-laying and following behaviour of ants.

In AI, ant colony optimisation algorithms are used in network routing, task scheduling, and solving the travelling salesman problem, showcasing efficiency in finding optimal solutions. For example, a delivery company can use AI algorithms based on ant colony behaviour to optimise delivery routes, minimising travel time and fuel consumption. This echoes the ants' efficient pathfinding strategies.

Bee Foraging and Decision Making

Honeybees use a democratic-like process to make group decisions about new nesting locations. Scout bees perform a 'waggle dance' to communicate the location and quality of potential sites. The intensity and duration of these dances influence colony decision making, exemplifying an algorithmic approach to collaborative decision making and consensus building.

This algorithm underscores the power of collective intelligence and democratic decision making. AI can adopt similar strategies for distributed problem solving and consensus building in areas like blockchain technology, swarm robotics, and collaborative filtering in recommendation systems.

Predator-Prey Dynamics

In ecosystems, the interactions between predators and prey follow certain patterns that can be modelled algorithmically. The Lotka-Volterra equations, for example, describe the cyclical fluctuations in predator and prey populations.[16]

The Lotka-Volterra equations are like a mathematical game that tells us how animals that eat other animals and the animals they eat live together in nature. These equations show us that sometimes there are lots of animals that get eaten, so the animals that eat them grow in number too. But if there are too many predators, there won't be enough food for all of them, so their numbers go down. Then the cycle starts again, like a big game of nature tag. This natural balance ensures ecosystem sustainability.

The predictive power of these models can inform AI's understanding and management of complex systems. Applications include ecological modelling, resource management, and even financial market analysis, where understanding cyclical patterns is crucial.

Pack-Hunting Strategies in Wolves

One species of predator in particular, wolves, uses strategic, cooperative hunting techniques that maximise their chances of a successful hunt while minimising energy expenditure. This involves complex communication and role assignments within the pack, which follow a set of behavioural 'algorithms' to efficiently catch prey.

The coordinated approach of wolves can inspire AI in areas requiring teamwork and strategy, such as in autonomous vehicles, drone swarms for search and rescue operations, and collaborative multi-agent systems in robotics.

Tree Nutrient Distribution

Trees and other plants distribute nutrients in a way that maximises efficiency and growth. This is comparable to an algorithmic process where resources are allocated based on need and potential for growth. The root systems of trees, particularly in fungal networks like the mycorrhizae, also showcase a natural algorithm for sharing resources and communicating.

This natural algorithm highlights efficient resource allocation and networked communication. AI systems can learn from this to optimise resource distribution in networked systems, improve communication protocols, and develop robust, decentralised networks.

Cellular Automata in Shell Patterns

The intricate patterns on seashells are formed by cellular automata, which are simple rules repeated over time. These rules, comparable to an algorithm, dictate how cells (or pigments in the case of shells) change over time, leading to complex, beautiful patterns.

This concept can inspire AI in the field of procedural generation, where simple rules can create complex, scalable designs and patterns. Applications include computer graphics, architectural design, and generative art, where efficiency and creativity are crucial.

These examples show how nature, through evolutionary processes, has developed systems and behaviours that are efficient, purposeful, and adaptive. These natural algorithms can inspire sustainable, effective solutions in various fields, including computing, engineering, and environmental management.

Indigenous Wisdom

Indigenous knowledge systems stand as profound repositories of understanding, deeply rooted in the interconnectedness of life, community, and the natural world. These ancient yet ever-relevant perspectives offer invaluable insights for shaping the ethics of Artificial Intelligence in our modern era. They remind us that technology, at its best, is an extension of human values and aspirations, capable of serving society and the planet when guided by principles of care, guardianship, and collective thriving.

The Essence of Indigenous Wisdom

At the heart of many indigenous worldviews is the principle of interconnectedness—a recognition that all aspects of life are deeply intertwined. This concept, manifested in the Quechua ethos of 'Buen Vivir', or living well in harmony, underscores the importance of collective wellbeing over individual gain.[17]

This stands in stark contrast to the often compartmentalised, efficiency-driven approach of the contemporary tech landscape. Imagine, then, an AI ethics framework infused with the spirit of Buen Vivir, prioritising technologies that foster societal and environmental harmony.

> Tune in to episode 64 of the *Amplify AI* podcast to listen to the really thought-provoking conversation I had with Neil Sahota about the ethical considerations of AI. He mentioned the story of a guy in Canada who used AI to create child pornography. It was a disturbing example, but it showed the potential for misuse and the importance of being proactive.

Neil also brought up an important point about how we often focus on the negative risks of AI while neglecting the positive potential.

For example, he noted, autonomous vehicles could save millions of lives each year by reducing car accidents. It's important to consider the full picture and understand the positive impact AI can have on society.

Principles of Care and Guardianship

The indigenous principles of manaakitanga (caring), kaitiakitanga (guardianship), and aloha 'āina (love for the land), from Māori and Native Hawaiian thought, provide a blueprint for developing AI that serves the common good.[18] These principles emphasise the role of AI as a steward, not merely as a tool for exploitation or profit.

An AI grounded in manaakitanga would prioritise empathy and care in its interactions, while one built on kaitiakitanga would safeguard digital and natural ecosystems for future generations.

Sovereignty and Stewardship over Data

The First Nations Information Governance Centre's OCAP principles (ownership, control, access, and possession) offer a robust model for asserting data rights, reflecting a broader call for sovereignty and stewardship in digital realms. These principles have already influenced policy in Canada, showcasing how indigenous governance concepts can shape national and global discussions on data ethics.

Similarly, the Māori Data Sovereignty Network's work with New Zealand's government on AI procurement policies exemplifies the potential for indigenous wisdom to inform equitable and culturally sensitive AI practices.

> In episode 64 of the *Amplify AI* podcast, Neil Sahota spoke about the importance of recapturing ancient wisdom, especially when it comes to collaboration. He used the example of a doctor who misdiagnosed a patient because he was too focused on a particular symptom. This highlights the need for us to be more open-minded and consider different perspectives when using AI.

It's not about replacing doctors or nurses, but about using AI to augment their intelligence and provide them with additional data points to help make more-informed decisions. AI can help us be more human, not less. That's a powerful idea.

Indigenous Authority and Digital Spaces

Initiatives like the Inuit Circumpolar Council's Pikialasorsuaq Declaration and the Aboriginal Territories in Cyberspace project highlight the critical need for indigenous voices in shaping the digital landscape.[20]

These efforts assert indigenous authority over data and digital spaces, advocating for a model of technological development that respects indigenous rights, values, and participation. It's a call for a digital ecosystem where indigenous communities are not mere subjects of data collection, but active designers of their digital futures.

Integrating Indigenous Practices with Technology

Projects such as the Ogimaa Mikana and collaborations by the Wikwemikong Tourism Department with researchers to create AI systems reflecting indigenous cultural values illustrate the fertile ground for innovation at the intersection of indigenous wisdom and technology.[21]

These initiatives demonstrate how AI can be thoughtfully integrated with indigenous practices to enhance community wellbeing, cultural preservation, and environmental stewardship.

One example of this is how indigenous communities in North America are using AI to help revitalise their languages by creating tools that translate and teach language to younger generations, therefore preserving cultural heritage. This aligns with indigenous values of cultural preservation and the ethical use of AI to empower communities.

Towards a New Paradigm of AI Ethics

Drawing on indigenous wisdom to inform AI usage and ethics represents a paradigm shift—from viewing AI as a tool for dominance and profit to seeing it as a partner in nurturing life, culture, and the planet. It encourages us to reimagine AI development as an inclusive process that honours the diversity of human perspectives, prioritises the collective good, and embraces the principles of care, guardianship, and sustainable coexistence.

Certain Australian indigenous wisdom, encapsulating the symbology of natural elements, offers an instructive lens through which to view the ethical integration of AI within the realm of business. Just as the natural world maintains a delicate balance through the interplay of forces, so too must AI operate within the bounds of ethical consideration, ensuring its power is harnessed for the collective betterment rather than individual gain.

Freshwater wisdom, with its emphasis on reflection and depth, serves as a reminder that the true value of AI lies beneath its surface capabilities. It implores us to consider AI not just as a tool for efficiency, but as a means for deeper understanding—to probe beneath the data and algorithms, and to discern the long-term ramifications of our technological endeavours. Just as fresh water sustains life and remains fluid despite the obstacles in its path, AI must sustain and enhance human life, providing adaptive solutions that flow with the ethical complexities of our world.

Saltwater wisdom celebrates the principle of adaptability—the capacity to navigate the ceaseless tides of change. In the context of AI, this translates to systems that are robust yet flexible, able to ride the waves of technological advancement while being anchored by a steadfast commitment to ethical practices. Like salt water, which shapes coastlines and sustains ecosystems, AI should shape industry landscapes and sustain societal structures with an inherent fluidity that allows for the evolution of its purpose and functions.

Desert wisdom teaches us about resilience and the importance of clarity amidst illusions. In business AI, this wisdom encourages the creation of systems that withstand the arid spells of innovation—the hype cycles and inflated expectations—and instead focus on creating value that endures. AI must be a mirage buster, peeling away the veneer of grandiose promises to reveal the core of what is truly beneficial for society, ensuring that every innovation is rooted in reality and serves a meaningful purpose.

Rainforest wisdom speaks to the rich interconnectedness inherent in the most biodiverse ecosystems on Earth. It compels us to envision AI as a facilitator of interconnected growth, where technology is not an isolating force but a connective tissue that binds various aspects of business and society. AI should foster a collaborative spirit, uniting different stakeholders, bridging gaps between disciplines, and cultivating an environment where collective intelligence flourishes.

In synthesising these elements, AI in business becomes a pursuit that seeks to automate and optimise, doing so with a consciousness that mirrors the most venerable aspects of our natural world. This ties in with Dr David Hawkins' Map of Consciousness, which we explored in Part 1.[22]

The implementation of AI, inspired by the principles of freshwater, saltwater, desert, and rainforest wisdom, becomes an exercise in creating technology that is as life-affirming as the ecosystems it emulates. It champions an AI that is ethical, empathetic, resilient, and collaborative, ensuring that the legacy of our technological advancements is as enduring and harmonious as the ancient wisdom that guides them.

With these principles as an example, business leaders are called upon to utilise AI in a manner where technology and ethics are interwoven, leading to a future where our digital advancements are as respected and integral to our society as the timeless teachings of indigenous wisdom.

Implementing Indigenous-Informed AI Ethics

To operationalise these insights, business leaders and AI developers can adopt several strategies:

1 **Inclusive Design Processes**: Engage with indigenous communities from the outset of AI projects to ensure technologies reflect and respect indigenous values and rights. This includes co-designing AI systems that embody principles like Buen Vivir, manaakitanga, and kaitiakitanga.

2 **Cultural Competency in AI Development**: Train AI developers and designers in cultural competency to appreciate the depth and diversity of indigenous knowledge systems. This can promote AI solutions that are not only technologically innovative, but also culturally sensitive and ethically grounded.

3 **Policy Advocacy for Indigenous Data Sovereignty**: Support and advocate for policies that recognise and protect indigenous data sovereignty, ensuring indigenous communities have control over how data about them is collected, used, and shared.

4 **Sustainable AI Practices**: Embrace AI development practices that are environmentally sustainable and aligned with the principle of aloha 'āina, reinforcing the critical relationship between technological advancement and planetary health.

5 **Community-Driven AI Applications:** Prioritise AI projects that address specific needs and aspirations of indigenous communities, such as revitalising languages, protecting traditional knowledge, and enhancing local economies.

By weaving indigenous wisdom into the fabric of AI ethics, we train technologies that are intelligent—capable of serving humanity's deepest needs for connection, stewardship, and harmony. These values are reflected in the next chapter, where I outline the five ethical parameters to consider when adopting AI. I call this the SymbioEthical Framework.

Let this be our guiding star: an AI ethics framework that, in its structure and spirit, celebrates the richness of human diversity and the sacredness of all life. In doing so, we honour the past, enrich the present, and seed a future where technology amplifies our collective quest for a just, sustainable, and flourishing world.

CHAPTER 6

THE SYMBIOETHICAL FRAMEWORK

AI is the ultimate catalyst for change.
Embrace it, experiment with it, and
let it drive your business forward.

N THE last chapter, I introduced you to various approaches that can help us decipher ethics when it comes to AI adoption. I want to highlight next the triad of intelligence. This speaks to the harmony of human, artificial, and divine intelligence—a symphony of capabilities that, when aligned, can produce outcomes far greater than the sum of their parts. This is a call to recognise and respect the unique contributions of each form of intelligence, ensuring they work in concert to achieve ethical, sustainable, and meaningful goals.

Now, I know 'divine intelligence' might sound a bit out there. But trust me on this one. It's not about religion or dogma; it's about those universal principles that resonate with all of us—compassion, empathy, fairness, a sense of purpose that transcends individual goals.

Tune in to the *Amplify AI* podcast episodes with Kylie Ryan to go deeper into divine intelligence.

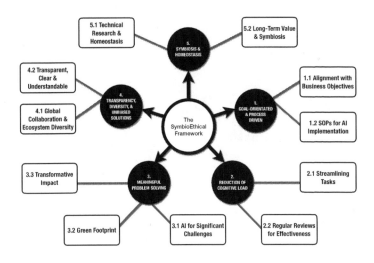

For business leaders, this means adopting AI in a way that complements and enhances human intelligence, as opposed to replacing it. It's about leveraging AI to tackle problems beyond our reach, while also ensuring that these technologies are guided by a moral compass, reflective of our highest ideals and aspirations. This triad of intelligence is not just a framework for technological integration, but a blueprint for a future where technology amplifies our humanity, rather than diminishing it.

The IEEE's 'Ethically Aligned Design' principles are the foundational pillars guiding us through this ethical AI technological advancement.[23] Just as sailors of old relied on celestial wisdom passed down to them, we can steer our AI integration process using this ethical constellation. And no one is more credible than the IEEE.

In crafting this SymbioEthical Framework, I've woven the threads of these universal ethics into a framework that reflects our deepest values. The IEEE emphasises human rights, wellbeing, data control, and responsibility, mirroring our commitment to creating AI that enhances human dignity and freedom.

Integrating these principles, let's imagine an AI designed not just to learn and predict but to understand and respect. A system that sees data not as mere bytes but as fragments of human stories, deserving of privacy and control. This is the AI we aim to build.

As I present you the parameters in this framework, let's remember that the goal isn't just to create AI that is intelligent but to craft technology that is wise. Wisdom comes from understanding the impact of our creations and committing to a path that respects the planet and its inhabitants. The IEEE principles, embedded within our framework, serve as a guide to this wisdom, helping us navigate AI with ethical integrity and a profound sense of purpose.

Five ethical parameters make up the SymbioEthical Framework. Each of the ethical parameters has sub-parameters that need to be achieved. There are a total of eleven sub-parameters. These unfold as follows:

1　Goal-Orientated and Process-Driven
1.1 Alignment with Business Objectives
1.2 SOPS for AI implementation

2　Reduction of Cognitive Load
2.1 Streamlining Tasks
2.2 Regular Reviews for Effectiveness

3　Meaningful Problem Solving
3.1 AI for Significant Challenges
3.2 Green Footprint
3.3 Transformative Impact

Let's look at each of these parameters in detail.

1. Goal-Orientated and Process-Driven

Imagine starting a hike without a map or a destination in mind. You may enjoy the scenery, but chances are you'll end up lost, right? That's precisely what happens when businesses implement AI without aligning it with their core goals and processes.

For example, a company might invest in a sophisticated AI-powered marketing tool without first defining their target audience or understanding their customer journey. Without this alignment, the tool becomes a shiny new toy that doesn't actually move the needle for the business.

In contrast, when you embrace a goal-orientated and process-driven approach, it's like having a GPS for your 'AI hike'. You know where you're headed and the best route to get there, ensuring that AI enhances your existing workflows and propels you towards your strategic objectives.

The AI world is moving at warp speed. If your business isn't evolving just as quickly, you're going to get left in the dust. Cameron Herold, who's worked with countless successful CEOs, says it best in episode 73 of the *Amplify AI* podcast: 'If the rate of change outside your business is greater than the rate of change inside your business, you're out of business.' Harsh, but true. AI is the ultimate catalyst for change. Embrace it, experiment with it, and let it drive your business forward.

1.1 Alignment with Business Objectives

Before Artificial Intelligence came along, as a business you ideated, planned, and projected your business objectives and goals. These still need to be the focus before adopting AI. Without this focus, using AI is just a fancy magic trick that looks cool, but does nothing to impact the business. In contrast, we're after the kind of magic that makes business objectives a reality.

Research emphasises the importance of aligning AI with business objectives for successful outcomes. In a study by Sado, Loo, Kerzel, and Wermter (2020), the authors put forward their view that the concept of explainable goal-driven agents in AI is crucial for transparency and trust in AI systems.[24] They introduce the idea of integrating eXplainable AI (XAI) principles. XAI will make AI's decision-making process transparent, fostering trust and ensuring alignment with business objectives. This is essential as AI systems should be able to justify their actions and decisions, especially in complex business environments.[24]

Ensure that all AI initiatives are in sync with the organisation's strategic goals. AI should enhance key business areas and contribute directly to achieving set objectives.

1.2 SOPs for AI Implementation

Integrating AI into an inefficient process will amplify its inefficiencies.

My thesis when I was completing my Master's in Software Engineering was on Process Quality. Process Quality is the simple idea that to measure the quality of software produced, you measure the quality of the process that goes into making and deploying that software. My thesis was one of the first research projects that merged the then rigid process quality framework of Capability Maturity Model Integration (CMMI) with the now widely accepted Agile process methodology.

CMMI is a quality framework used to audit and accredit software technology companies. ISO 9001 is a process framework to audit and accredit companies' quality management systems. Organisations use the ISO 9001 standard to demonstrate the ability to consistently provide products and services that meet customer and regulatory requirements. I have since helped to take two companies to their ISO 9001 accreditations using my thesis, acting as Lead Quality Auditor, so you can trust me when I tell you: Process is everything.

Develop and adhere to Standard Operating Procedures for AI development and deployment. These SOPs should reflect your organisation's ethos and mission, ensuring a consistent approach to AI integration.

2. Reduction of Cognitive Load

Ever tried multitasking during a busy day and ended up feeling more frazzled than productive? That's exactly what happens when you're overloaded with too much to do. And it's an example of cognitive overload.

In the business world, overloading teams with complex tasks is like expecting someone to juggle flaming torches while balancing on a unicycle. It's not just daunting; it's downright risky!

Now, consider using AI to take over those repetitive, mind-numbing tasks. It's like having a personal assistant who's always on the ball, giving you the freedom to focus on what truly matters. Let me talk about a recent example of implementing this for my book writing project.

When Sara, my editor, read the first draft of my manuscript, she made changes and suggested a lot of improvements (seventeen pages of them). So, I created my own AI to go through the edited draft of my manuscript and all my editor's suggestions. I asked this AI to organise the tasks there were to do, ranked by their difficulty to complete. And then I asked it to not show me the whole list, but just the next suggestion to tackle. When I completed something from the list I asked my AI to mark it as complete. Then, at the end of the day, I asked my AI for a productivity report. What did I complete and what was coming up? Talk about freeing up cognitive load to just write, rather than organise what task to do next.

You have to be careful, though. If you rely too much on AI, you might lose touch with your team. The key is finding that sweet spot where AI complements human efforts without overshadowing them. Consider an accounting firm implementing AI software to automate data entry and reconciliation tasks. This frees up their accountants to focus on higher-level analysis and client consultation, reducing their mental workload and enhancing job satisfaction.

Adopted in an ethical way, AI can prompt users to engage more actively in decision-making processes, preserving human cognitive skills and preventing overreliance or skill atrophy.

Cognitive load reduction through AI is supported by research. A study on human-AI symbiosis by Becks and Weis (2022) discusses the balance to be struck where AI assists humans without causing dependency or skill loss.[25] The idea here is to implement nudging mechanisms in AI. This approach maintains a healthy balance between human intuition and AI assistance.

2.1 Streamlining Tasks

As a business, knowing how much effort goes into your major activities helps reduce workload and increases efficiency. Design AI to take over complex or repetitive tasks, thereby reducing the cognitive load on humans. Focus on enhancing efficiency and user experience.

The Industrial Age helped us streamline tasks to create an efficient production line. We got better at mechanising things. As a human species, what we achieved due to the Industrial Age is the foundation upon which the Information and Intelligence Age have come about. So streamlining is key.

Remember this sequence for best results. Streamline activities, feed in the right information, and apply the right intelligence to get the best results.

2.2 Regular Reviews for Effectiveness

Conduct periodic assessments to ensure AI systems are effectively reducing workload without introducing undue stress or creating dependencies.

As a team, decide what methods you can use to measure success in terms of effectiveness. A company that cares about its people may find a way to achieve their business goals with AI and allow their people more time off.

Regularly assessing the impact you are creating helps a business progress towards the impact it wants to create, in line with its values.

3. Meaningful Problem Solving

Have you ever seen someone use a hammer to fix a computer? Absurd, right? That's what it's like when businesses use AI without focusing on meaningful problem solving.

They might be hammering away with good intentions, but the problems just get worse. Ignoring this parameter leads to misusing AI. Like using a chainsaw to carve a turkey, it's overkill and ineffective. This parameter is about choosing the right tool for the job.

Think about a team using AI to study climate change and figure out what's going to happen next. This is a prime example of AI being directed towards a significant, real-world problem with far-reaching consequences. It's about choosing the right tool for the job—and using that tool to make a positive impact on the world.

When you use AI to solve real problems, it's like a surgeon using a scalpel—precise, effective, and life-changing. That said, beware the pitfalls. Don't get so caught up in solving problems that you forget who you're solving them for. Keep it human-centric. After all, what good is a solution if it doesn't resonate with the people it's meant to help?

We need to use AI to make the world a better place, both for people and the environment. This aligns AI initiatives with global sustainability goals and ethical standards, ensuring long-term benefits for both business and society.[26]

3.1 AI for Significant Challenges

As a business, imagine solving significant challenges that are outside your current capability.

When I was training to be a chef, my head chef Dan told me something that I will forever remember. At the time, he was teaching me to use a knife efficiently. This is one of the first tasks you learn as a chef (after you learn how to wash dishes and clean the kitchen after service). When you're learning to be proficient with your knife, you are given massive amounts of ingredients to cut. This has to be done efficiently and the cuts all have to be equal.

One day I was tasked with cutting twenty-five kilograms of cabbage for sauerkraut. While he was guiding me, Dan said, 'Ronsley, if you're trying to solve a problem that can be solved in your lifetime, then you're thinking too small.' I've taken that idea into everything I've achieved since, and I'd love for you to do the same.

Direct AI efforts towards solving critical, real-world problems. Ensure that the problems addressed are relevant, impactful, and aligned with your organisation's mission and society's needs.

3.2 Green Footprint

This parameter highlights the importance of checking what impact your business goals could have on the planet. Without this consideration, we could achieve the business's goals while harming people, other living things, and whole ecosystems.

In the course of writing this book, I interviewed several indigenous elders from different parts of the world. One conversation I can't forget was with an Inuit lady. She said to me halfway through our conversation, 'So, Ronsley, if you're saying that Artificial Intelligence is going to be the biggest conversation of our lifetime, then how does it affect my relative the beaver? And my relative the bear? And my relative the tree?'

'We have to consider the effects of what we are doing,' she told me, 'especially for the ones that don't have a voice.'

My friend Gary Vaynerchuk, one of the most influential entrepreneurs on the planet, sees it the same way. He's been talking about the power of AI with me on the podcast (tune in to episode 50 to listen), and he's right—it's already changing the game. It's reshaping how we work, connect, and create.

Here's the catch: if we're not ready to use it in the right way, AI might not give us much choice. It could easily overtake some of the things we do and change the world as we know it. That's why we need to start thinking about how to use AI ethically, with empathy, and with a deep understanding of our values. We must learn from ancient wisdom and embrace a more collaborative approach.

Think about it this way: AI is a powerful tool, but it's only as good as the data it's fed. So if we want AI to work for us, we need to make sure that data reflects our best values. And guess what? The easiest way to do that is to use empathy.

That's right—empathy is your secret weapon in the age of AI. Gary Vee has been talking about this for years, and he's right: understanding and caring for your audience is crucial for navigating the complexities of AI adoption.

It's about stepping into their shoes, understanding their needs and desires, and using AI to help them reach their goals. It's about being more than just a vendor or a provider—it's about being a guide and a partner. AI can be your most powerful growth tool, but only if you approach it with empathy.

Develop AI with a focus on promoting fairness and reducing environmental impacts. Incorporate eco-friendly practices in AI development and deployment. Regularly assess and adjust AI systems to ensure they contribute positively to social equity and ecological balance.

3.3 Transformative Impact

I believe that businesses are created to solve meaningful problems for their audiences. It is a business's responsibility to focus on the delivery of this transformation for its audience in a way that impacts them positively. These days a lot of social media accounts are making promises that they can't keep just to get their audience to click on their posts. It's the same with ads, podcasts, and YouTube videos. Creators are writing titles for the click, and not focusing on the transformation they can provide.

If you started your business to help certain types of people, or in your marketing you highlight how your product or service can change someone's life, then using AI to dramatically improve their situation feels like something basic every leader would want to explore. With AI we can actually deliver on all the amazing promises we make as leaders.

Aim for AI solutions that create broader positive changes beyond their immediate application. Encourage innovation that leads to transformative benefits for users and society.

4. Transparency, Diversity, and Unbiased Solutions

Imagine trying to complete a puzzle with half the pieces missing. Frustrating, isn't it? When you don't think about transparency and diversity, you're missing a big part of that puzzle picture. You end up with a solution that's as clear as mud and as biased as a crooked referee. The consequences? Mistrust, misinterpretation, and a one-sided AI that echoes only a fraction of the voices it should represent.

Think about a software company developing facial recognition technology. If they only use data from a limited demographic, their system might be biased and inaccurate for other groups. But if they actively seek diverse datasets and audit their algorithms for bias, they can ensure their system is fair and accurate across different demographics. This promotes inclusivity and ethical use, making AI a force for good, not a source of discrimination.

Now, imagine an AI that's as diverse as a city street—full of different voices and perspectives. It's like having a chorus where every voice is heard, and every note is crystal clear. But it's a delicate balance. Too much transparency can lead to information overload, and diversity for diversity's sake is like a salad with too many ingredients—confusing and unpalatable. The trick is to mix the right elements for a solution that's both understandable and representative.

The necessity to foster transparent, diverse, and unbiased AI solutions is found in research. A study led by Ntoutsi (2020) on bias in data-driven AI systems highlights the importance of designing inclusive AI that avoids discriminatory practice.[27]

Establish rigorous bias detection and mitigation processes, because by actively identifying and mitigating biases, you ensure that AI systems are fair and inclusive. This also involves building diverse teams that can provide varied perspectives, making AI systems more representative and equitable.[27]

4.1 Global Collaboration and Ecosystem Diversity

Involve diverse teams in AI development to capture a broad range of perspectives. This diversity can lead to more inclusive and effective AI solutions.

ChatGPT already has bias built into it. Actually, most Large Language Models (LLMs) do. Especially if the model was originally trained by scraping the internet. That is why when you talk to ChatGPT in British English, it will reply in American English. Most training data was written in American English.

Remember that people who conquered and triumphed over other people have written most of our captured history. How much history has been captured, stored, and remembered by the original and indigenous peoples of Australia, America, Asia, India, and Africa? We've seen the destruction of the cultures and wisdom of these people. Let's not take that injustice into our development of and dealings with AI.

4.2 Transparent, Clear, and Understandable Solutions

Implement transparent AI systems where decision-making processes are clear and understandable.

AI solutions must be available to everyone, not only a select few. They should also be understandable, usable, and transparent. The way AI is used must be a company-wide decision. What guardrails need to be determined and abided by? This is too powerful a sub-parameter to be ignored.

5. Symbiosis and Homeostasis

Homeostasis is how all living things (including your body!) regulate themselves. It's how they keep their insides stable, regardless of what's happening on the outside, adjusting external changes whenever they need to. As for symbiosis—have you ever seen those nature shows where animals help each other out? That's symbiosis—where close association benefits everyone. If one thing takes over, things get messed up. That's what happens when AI isn't balanced with humans. That's the business landscape without a focus on symbiosis and homeostasis in AI. It leads to a lopsided ecosystem where either technology overshadows humanity or vice versa, disrupting the balance.

Think about a manufacturing company that uses AI to optimise production processes. They could just replace all their workers with robots, right? But that could lead to job losses and societal unrest. Instead, they choose to use AI to enhance their workers' capabilities, providing them with tools and insights to make their jobs safer and more efficient. This creates a symbiotic relationship where technology and humans work together in harmony, achieving a balance that benefits everyone.

Mahmud, Hong, and Fong's 2022 research on human-AI symbiosis for creative work discusses the potential of AI and humans working together effectively.[28] The upshot is that AI systems should be developed with the capability to complement human skills, ensuring a balanced and mutually beneficial relationship. This approach leverages the strengths of both humans and AI, leading to more effective and creative problem solving.

> This makes me think of Kylie Ryan's powerful statement on the *Amplify AI* podcast: 'AI might be the very thing that helps us rebalance our world from this overly masculine world into a more balanced world, if we can trust it.' This is the kind of symbiosis we're talking about. Tune in to episode 84 for the full conversation.

5.1 Technical Research and Homeostasis

I've always found the line 'ignorance is not a defence' very inspiring. Especially in today's social media world, where most people with an account have an uninformed opinion about most things. Though I spend a lot of my time in the AI space, I still feel like there's more to learn, despite having read hundreds of research papers, led multiple companies to develop quality processes, and written and sold my own AI tool. The more I learn, the more I realise I don't know. Especially when it comes to Artificial Intelligence.

Writing this book has taken more than eighteen months. Over a year of that time involved a literature review to read and learn about what others have done in the space, so that

I could build on existing knowledge. That's on top of over thirty years of computing experience and nine years at university (four years for my Bachelor's in Computer Science and Engineering, three years for my Master's in Software Engineering, and another two years for my Master's in Business Administration, majoring in Psychology and Leadership). This has all taught me the value of technical research and the importance of learning for adapting to change, technological or otherwise.

Develop AI with an emphasis on stability and predictability. Ensure AI systems are robust, secure, and can adapt to changing conditions while maintaining operational integrity. Regularly review AI performance to ensure it maintains equilibrium in various scenarios.

5.2 Long-Term Value and Symbiosis

Design AI solutions that benefit both the organisation and society over the long term. Encourage AI applications that enhance user experience and societal welfare, and contribute to sustainable development. Measure the long-term impact of AI projects on both the organisation and the community.

As a business, avoiding being parasitic by nature while offering long-term value will garner your business a lot of trust. Your brand's equity will only go up.

Here we've laid out the five core parameters of the SymbioEthical Framework—our compass for navigating the ethical complexities of AI. But a compass is only as good as the navigator who wields it. As business leaders, it's our responsibility to ensure this framework is woven into every decision we make, every initiative we launch, and every interaction we have with AI.

This means asking tough questions: Does this AI application align with our business goals and values? Is it truly reducing cognitive load without creating unhealthy dependencies? Are we addressing meaningful problems, or are we just chasing shiny objects? Are our AI solutions transparent, diverse, and unbiased? And are we fostering a symbiotic relationship with AI, one where technology enhances our humanity, rather than replacing it?

Answering these questions honestly and thoughtfully is the first step towards a future where AI is a force for good in the world. Next, in Part 3, we'll explore a practical framework—the Amplify AI Pyramid—that will guide you to implement AI effectively, ensuring that every step you take is aligned with both your business objectives and your ethical compass.

PART 3

THE AMPLIFY AI PYRAMID

CHAPTER 7

HOW TO DECIPHER THE AMPLIFY AI PYRAMID

Incorporating AI into your strategy for audience growth is a transformative move. It's about embracing the complexity of human connection in the digital space and using the tools of tomorrow to foster bonds that are genuine and enduring.

THE AMPLIFY AI Pyramid sounds fancy, right? It's like having a blueprint for building a business powered by AI, but with a heart. This isn't about chasing profits; it's about making a real difference. I've seen first-hand how this framework can transform companies, helping them grow with purpose.

The pyramid can be viewed from different perspectives. Each view shows you a different way to use AI that will save time and money (and even reputation!) for your business. We'll go through these various perspectives before examining how to integrate AI into your business step by step, using the pyramid.

The Outcome for Your Business

Imagine what impact your business will have made in your life, your audience's lives, and the lives of your partners in ten years' time. What is your ten-year vision?

What would your business look like if you used AI ethically to grow revenue, brand, audience, and operations to amplify profit, trust, impact and legacy? This is why business leaders are so valuable. They imagine an outcome for the future and then lead their people to achieve that vision.

Articulate the outcome you will strive to have for your business ten years from now. Once you have this on paper, I'm going to show you how to get to that outcome in the coming chapters.

The 2 Axes

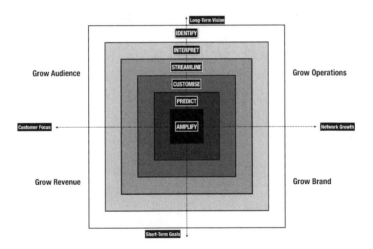

This is the pyramid viewed from above, and before we get to the front view the two axes are important. Because once you've homed in on what your outcome looks like, there are only two key things you as a business leader need to achieve. The first is a breakdown of your vision, including the points at which you are going to achieve the different milestones on your way to your ten-year outcome. The second is reach— the buy-in that your vision needs to attract along the way.

1. Vision

The Y-axis is your company's vision. This spans from your short-term goals at the bottom of the axis to your long-term vision at the top of the axis.

2. Reach

The X-axis is your company's reach. The X-axis shows how your reach expands—from your customers to your entire network.

With those axes in mind, we're going to look at the front view of the pyramid and its six steps first, before coming back to the top view and tackling each of the quadrants of the pyramid in turn, applying the six steps to the four main business areas (revenue, brand, audience, and operations) in the coming chapters.

Front View

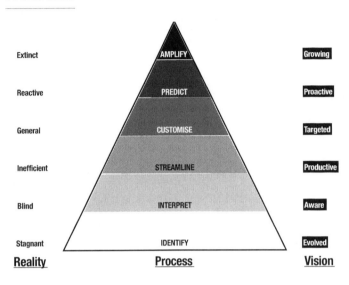

Reality	Process	Vision
Extinct	AMPLIFY	Growing
Reactive	PREDICT	Proactive
General	CUSTOMISE	Targeted
Inefficient	STREAMLINE	Productive
Blind	INTERPRET	Aware
Stagnant	IDENTIFY	Evolved

Step 1: Identify

This step is like building the foundation for AI—it's about making sure AI is aligned with your brand and goals. Starting this process with the right intention and focus is important. Think of the parent who leads by example rather than by giving orders to 'correct' behaviour. This step emphasises the crucial role of leadership in guiding AI's development ethically and responsibly. Just as a parent imparts wisdom and values to their children, business leaders must nurture AI with the same level of integrity and foresight.

This involves embedding ancestral wisdom and ethical principles into AI systems. It's about teaching AI the right way to act, making sure it's ethical and good for everyone. This makes people trust you and makes sure AI is working for your company's goals, ensuring its power is used for the greater good. It's about guiding ethical AI use, demonstrating how technology should support humanity's progress.

There are four main tasks to address to complete the Identify step:

1 **Identify Your Brand's Identity**: Understand and articulate what your brand stands for.

2 **Identify Your Business's Vision and Impact**: Clarify your long-term vision and the impact you seek.

3 **Identify Your Business's Methods**: Determine how your business fulfils its brand promise.

4 **Identify Your Business's Goals**: Set clear, measurable goals.

Implementation: Get your team together and talk it through. Ask them what they think, you know? Surveys are helpful too. Don't be wishy-washy. Make sure everything lines up with what your company believes in.

Ethical parameters to consider in this step:

1.1—Alignment with Business Objectives: Ensure that all AI initiatives are in sync with the organisation's strategic goals. AI should enhance key business areas and contribute directly to achieving set objectives.

4.2—Transparent, Clear and Understandable Solutions: Implement transparent AI systems where decision-making processes are clear and understandable.

Step 2: Interpret

This step is important because it offers deep insights into the operational and audience aspects identified in Step 1. In this step we clarify and validate what we've identified in the previous step.

Tasks:

1 **Interpret Your Brand's Guidelines**: Review and understand your brand's guiding principles.

2 **Interpret Your Audience's WHY Stack**: Analyse the motivations and behaviours of your audience.

3 **Interpret Your Business's Operational Blocks**: Identify operational challenges and strengths.

4 **Interpret Your Business's Vital Signs**: Assess key performance indicators. I call these vital signs. These feature in weekly reports analysing new listeners, new leads, new appointments, new presentations, new sales, and new partnerships.

Implementation: Use the four tasks identified in Step 1 to enable detailed analysis in this step. Use the brand identity to interpret the brand's guidelines. Use the business goals to interpret its vital signs. Use identified business methods to interpret operational blocks to consider. Use the vision of your business to interpret your audience's WHY stack to understand their motivations, desires, and challenges (we'll cover how to do this later in the book). Double-check your findings with real-world data, just to make sure you're on the right track.

Ethical parameters to consider for this step:

1.1—Alignment with Business Objectives: Ensure that all AI initiatives are in sync with the organisation's strategic goals. AI should enhance key business areas and contribute directly to achieving set objectives.

4.1—Global Collaboration and Ecosystem Diversity: Involve diverse teams in AI development to capture a broad range of perspectives. This diversity can lead to more inclusive and effective AI solutions.

Step 3: Streamline

The importance of this step lies in its focus on enhancing efficiency and productivity.

Tasks:

1 **Streamline Your Brand's Channels**: Optimise communication and distribution channels.

2 **Streamline Your Audience's Attention**: Capture and maintain audience interest effectively.

3 **Streamline Your Business's SOPs**: Refine standard operating procedures.

4 **Streamline Your Product Sales**: Improve sales processes.

Implementation: Get your processes running smoothly before you start automating stuff. Make sure you're not missing anything important.

Ethical parameters to consider for this step:

2.1—Streamlining Tasks: Design AI to take over complex or repetitive tasks, thereby reducing cognitive load on humans. Focus on enhancing efficiency and user experience.

1.2—SOPs for AI Implementation: Develop and adhere to Standard Operating Procedures for AI development and deployment. These SOPs should reflect your organisation's ethos and mission, ensuring a consistent approach to AI integration.

Step 4: Customise

This step is about building a closer connection with your audience by personalising their experiences.

Tasks:

1 **Customise Your Brand's Templates**: Tailor communication templates to various audience segments.

2 **Customise Your Audience's Engagement**: Personalise engagement strategies.

3 **Customise Your AI Solutions**: Adapt AI tools to specific business needs.

4 **Customise Your Sales Conversions**: Personalise sales approaches for higher conversion.

Implementation: Use AI to make things personal, but be careful not to violate anyone's privacy.
Ethical parameters to consider in this step:

3.1—AI for Significant Challenges: Direct AI efforts towards solving critical, real-world problems. Ensure that the problems addressed are relevant, impactful, and align with your organisation's mission and society's needs.

5.1—Technical Research and Homeostasis: Develop AI with an emphasis on stability and predictability. Ensure AI systems are robust, secure, and can adapt to changing conditions while maintaining operational integrity. Regularly review AI performance to ensure it maintains equilibrium in various scenarios.

Step 5: Predict

This step shifts the business from being reactive to being proactive, building credibility.
Tasks:

1 **Predict Partnerships**: Identify potential strategic alliances.

2 **Predict New Markets**: Forecast market trends and opportunities.

3 **Predict Reduction of Cognitive Load**: Anticipate and address workforce challenges.

4 **Predict Revenue Opportunities**: Identify emerging revenue streams.

Implementation: Utilise predictive analytics. Use AI to see what's coming, but don't treat it like a crystal ball. Think of it as a roadmap.
Ethical parameters to consider for this step:

3.2—Green Footprint: Develop AI with a focus on promoting fairness and reducing environmental impacts. Incorporate eco-friendly practices in AI development and deployment. Regularly assess and adjust AI systems to ensure they contribute positively to social equity and ecological balance.

5.2—Long-term Value and Symbiosis: Design AI solutions that benefit both the organisation and society over the long term. Encourage AI applications that enhance user experience and societal welfare, and contribute to sustainable development. Measure the long-term impact of AI projects on both the organisation and the community.

Step 6: Amplify
This final step drives growth and ensures the longevity of the business.
Tasks:

1 **Amplify Trust**: Strengthen trust with stakeholders.

2 **Amplify Impact**: Increase the positive impact of your business on your people.

3 **Amplify Legacy**: Build a lasting brand legacy.

4 **Amplify Profit**: Maximise profit in sustainable ways.

Implementation: Think about how you can grow your business, but don't sacrifice your values to do it.
Ethical parameters to consider for this step:

3.3—Transformative Impact: Aim for AI solutions that create broader positive changes beyond their immediate application. Encourage innovation that leads to transformative benefits for users and society.

2.2—Regular Reviews for Effectiveness: Conduct periodic assessments to ensure AI systems are effectively reducing workload without introducing undue stress or creating dependencies.

Top View

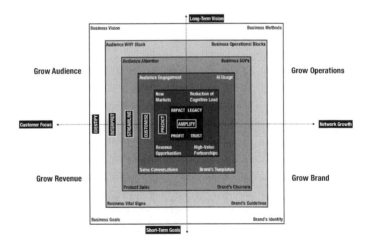

One of the best things my dad, Ricardo, said to me when I was very young was, 'Ronsley, loving a girl and living with a girl are two different things.' Just like using ChatGPT won't grow your business, and just like being on Facebook or having a podcast won't get you an audience. This pyramid offers you a framework to follow so you can actually achieve transformational outcomes.

A view of the Amplify AI Pyramid from the top shows each layer and how it relates to growing the four main business areas: revenue, brand, audience, and operations. These are the four growth quadrants.

Revenue Growth

This area focuses on increasing sales, profits, and overall revenue generation for your organisation. As a leader, your goal is to drive rapid yet sustainable top-line growth.

The Amplify AI Pyramid offers features like data-driven decision making, optimised sales processes, and personalised customer interactions to increase conversion rates and customer lifetime value. Key benefits include expanded partnerships and distribution channels along with amplified profits.

Potential mistakes like ineffective targeting, poor personalisation, and lack of sales optimisations can be avoided by following the strategic process outlined.

With this area done right, you'll achieve expanded networks and partnerships, higher conversion rates, and maximise revenue and profitability.

Brand Growth

This aspect concentrates on growing brand awareness, affinity, trust, and loyalty. Your leadership goal here is to amplify your brand's reputation and equity.

By ensuring any AI aligns with brand identity and values, features like tailored brand messaging and personalised customer experiences become possible. This builds loyalty by consistently meeting customer expectations.

Mistakes like impersonal campaigns, tone-deaf messaging, and misaligned experiences can be prevented through the framework's emphasis on brand consistency. Executed effectively, you'll see increased affinity and satisfaction from a customer base that recognises and values your distinct brand promise.

Audience Growth

The focus here is on sustaining and expanding your reach by deeply engaging your core audiences. Your objective as a leader is to maximise impact by fostering lasting audience relationships.

Powerful features include personalised interactions, predictive insights into audience needs, and well-timed communications. This results in benefits like sustained attention and amplified reach.

Pitfalls like superficial personalisation, neglecting insights, and poor timing are averted by following the prescribed process.

Done right, you'll forge lasting bonds with audiences, anticipate and meet their evolving needs through data-driven insights, and achieve greater impact over time.

Operations Growth

This sphere centres on optimising operations for productivity, efficiency, and innovation. Your leadership aim is to future-proof operations and build organisational resilience.

Key features are workforce augmentation, automation for efficiency gains, and predictive insights to guide planning. Benefits include increased productivity, reduced costs, and strategic agility.

The pyramid's six-step methodology prevents missteps like short-sighted automation, lack of augmentation, and ignored insights.

Implemented effectively, you'll achieve a future-ready organisation—nimble, efficient, and continuously optimising through AI integration.

Short-Term Goals and Long-Term Vision

In the Amplify AI Pyramid, we focus on revenue and brand as short-term goals. It's about laying a solid foundation—the kind that allows a business to make genuine impact, not just survive and get by. For a new business, or even a new product, amplifying revenue and solidifying a brand are essential first steps. They create the financial stability and market recognition that will fuel long-term growth. It's like building a house—you wouldn't start with the roof; you'd lay a strong foundation first. And just like any good foundation, it needs reinforcement. That's where trust comes in—amplifying your brand through consistent, ethical practices and authentic storytelling is key to capturing those all-important early wins.

However, to create a legacy, to truly amplify your impact, you need to shift your focus to the long term: your audience and your operations. That's why, in my first book, *AMPLIFY*, I dedicated an entire section to using a podcast to consistently engage and grow your audience. This approach, coupled with streamlining your internal processes, is what unlocks sustainable growth and positions you for long-term success. Just as a marathon runner needs endurance, building a lasting business requires a long-term vision, a commitment to your people (both your team and your audience), and a relentless pursuit of operational excellence.

Grow Revenue: Short-Term Goal—Customer Focus

The goal here is to leverage AI to use your customer's success stories and enhance revenue streams in the near term.

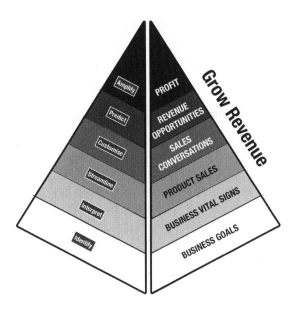

In the digital age, businesses are constantly seeking innovative ways to drive revenue growth. AI has brought a transformative shift in how businesses approach their growth strategies. However, tapping into this is not without its challenges. Usually, the issue at this stage is underestimating the knowledge required to execute this correctly. The Grow Revenue quadrant of the Amplify AI Pyramid serves as a guide, directing businesses through the noise, where 'everyone is a ChatGPT expert', towards an AI integration that increases profitability.

At the heart of revenue growth lies a complex puzzle that AI promises to solve: How can businesses scale up efficiently while maintaining or improving customer satisfaction? AI offers an array of solutions, from automating mundane tasks to delivering intricate customer insights, but leveraging these capabilities effectively is where many stumble.

When we are going after revenue as a business, we usually make three mistakes:

1. **We lack clear objectives**: Without crystal-clear goals, AI becomes a ship without a rudder—it may move but with no direction. Many businesses get into AI without defining what success looks like, leading to wasted investments and missed opportunities. With AI right now, you see a lot of great magic tricks, but those tricks don't actually grow the business.

2. **We mishandle data**: AI feeds on data, but if that data is flawed, the resulting decisions will be too. Businesses often neglect the need for a robust data strategy, resulting in AI systems that are as misguided as they are sophisticated. At the moment, many are guilty of feeding copyrighted data into open LLMs and using customer data without permission, all with good intent, but without ethical consideration.

3. **We underestimate our talent**: AI isn't self-sustaining; it requires skilled navigators. Companies frequently underestimate the need for talent that can bridge the gap between AI capabilities and business acumen. Training our teams to understand and use AI is one of the most impactful things we can do as business leaders.

To apply the Amplify AI strategy successfully, businesses must embrace certain core beliefs and values:

1. **Data Integrity**: Believe in the sanctity of data. Quality data is the lifeblood of AI, and ensuring its accuracy and relevance must be paramount.

2. **Ethical AI Use**: Adopt the values of the SymbioEthical Framework. AI should be used responsibly, with consideration for privacy, bias, and transparency.

3. **Long-Term Commitment**: View AI as a long-term partner in growth. The focus should be sustainable integration, not just short-term gains.

The Amplify AI Pyramid isn't just a structure; it's a philosophy. It encourages businesses to look beyond the allure of AI as a quick fix and instead see it as a strategic tool that, when aligned with business goals, can lead to exponential growth.

In the next chapter we will go into detail on how you apply the Amplify AI Pyramid to grow revenue.

Grow Brand: Short-Term Goal—Network Growth

The objective here is to focus on strengthening your brand's market position while growing your network through AI.

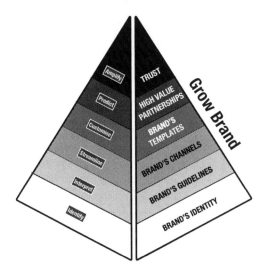

It's a tough world out there, but a strong brand can make all the difference. The 'Grow Brand' quadrant of the Amplify AI Pyramid serves as a compass, guiding our businesses through the digital landscape with a robust AI-powered approach. This is about flourishing in an era when brand identity and customer experience are king.

This section is about how to manage your brand in the age of AI. Brands need to adapt to a world where customer experiences are increasingly personalised and where engagement is both instantaneous and incessant. The challenge is managing this digital transformation without losing the essence of what makes your brand unique.

When we as business leaders try to grow the business's brand, we tend to make three mistakes:

1 **We overlook online reputation management**: One tweet can build or harm your brand online. Many companies find themselves overwhelmed by the sheer volume of online interactions, failing to leverage AI's potential to manage their online presence effectively.

2 **We pursue misguided audience connection efforts**: With the multitude of channels available, it's easy to lose sight of who your audience is and what they desire. Some brands continue to cast wide nets instead of using AI to connect with the right audience with precision and purpose.

3 **We neglect the customer experience**: Every customer interaction is an opportunity to reinforce your brand. Unfortunately, many businesses still don't utilise AI to its full potential, and miss out on chances to deepen customer relationships and loyalty.

To use the full power of AI in brand management, it's essential to embody certain beliefs and values:

1 **Commitment to Data Privacy**: In the era of general data protection regulation (GDPR) and increasing data breach concerns, brands must prioritise customer data security and privacy in all their AI initiatives.

2 **Transparency in AI Applications**: Make sure your customers understand how AI is helping them.

3 **Embrace of Continuous Learning**: The landscape is ever evolving, and so should be your brand's approach to AI. A commitment to ongoing learning and adaptation is crucial.

By integrating AI into your brand strategy using the Amplify AI Pyramid, you position your brand not just to meet the expectations of the digital age, but to set new standards. It's about evolving with grace, and embracing innovation without sacrificing the heart of your brand. Remember that your brand's story is still about connection—AI is simply the newest chapter that can enhance this experience.

We'll examine the six steps of the Amplify AI Pyramid in this quadrant in detail in their own chapter.

Grow Audience: Long-Term Vision—Customer Focus

The objective here is to expand the reach and engagement of the brand's audience, with a long-term vision that centres on customer needs and preferences.

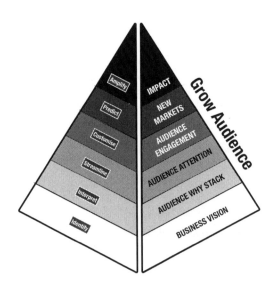

In the ever-evolving digital marketplace, the vitality of your audience can make or break your business. Building and nurturing an audience is an art form that requires finesse, insight, and the ability to adapt. The 'Grow Audience' quadrant of the Amplify AI Pyramid offers a strategic framework for leveraging Artificial Intelligence to grow and to deeply understand and engage with your audience.

The digital landscape is saturated with content, products, and services all vying for attention. The challenge is to not merely capture attention but transform it into lasting engagement. In this environment, the problem becomes one of connection—how do you resonate authentically with an audience bombarded with options?

As businesses we tend to make these three mistakes when trying to grow our audiences:

1 **We have undefined audience personas**: Many businesses cast a wide net, hoping to catch as many people as possible, but an undefined audience can lead to diluted messages and wasted resources.

2 **We ignore audience insights**: In the age of data, neglecting the rich insights available through AI can leave you disconnected from the evolving needs and behaviours of your audience.

3 **We uphold static engagement strategies**: What worked yesterday may not resonate today. Businesses that fail to adapt their engagement strategies to the dynamic digital ecosystem often find their audience slipping away.

To truly benefit from the Amplify AI strategy, your business must hold certain beliefs and values at its core:

1. **Dynamic Audience Understanding**: Your audience is not static; as their world changes, so do their needs and desires. Believe in the power of AI to keep a finger on your audience's pulse.

2. **Ethical Data Utilisation**: Trust is the currency of the digital age. Value your audience's privacy and use their data ethically, ensuring transparency in how it informs your strategies.

3. **Commitment to Innovation**: Embrace innovation as a constant, not a one-time initiative. Cultivate a culture of continuous learning and agility, with AI as your ally in audience growth.

Incorporating AI into your strategy for audience growth is a transformative move. It's about embracing the complexity of human connection in the digital space and using the tools of tomorrow to foster bonds that are genuine and enduring. With the Amplify AI Pyramid as your guide, you can chart a course to an engaged and loyal audience that will ensure your brand's success in the digital era.

We'll unpack the six steps towards revolutionising your connection with your audience in a later chapter.

Grow Operations: Long-Term Vision—Network Growth

The objective here is to enhance operational efficiency and agility with AI, allowing for sustainable growth and network expansion.

In the modern business landscape, operational growth is about more than scaling up; it's about scaling smart. The 'Grow Operations' quadrant of the Amplify AI Pyramid

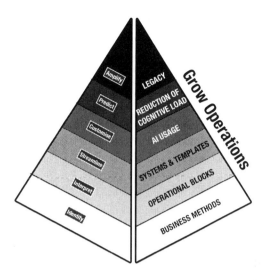

presents a strategic framework with which to leverage AI for operational excellence. This approach is about precision, efficiency, and future-proofing the heart of your business— its operations.

The challenge businesses face is twofold: integrating cutting-edge technology into existing processes and ensuring that this integration translates into tangible operational improvements.

As a qualified chef, I like nothing more than watching a busy kitchen in action with the menu in my hand. I am not looking at my menu to choose a dish to eat. For the last five years, I've always asked my waiter to recommend something and I eat whatever they recommend. I'm looking at the menu to reverse engineer what the head chef was thinking when she put that dish on the menu. What does her mise-en-place—her setup—look like? What are the roles of the different chefs preparing that dish? What cooking techniques are being used to prepare and plate this dish? It is the best orchestra I've experienced—a busy kitchen.

As businesses we tend to make three mistakes when we try to grow operations:

1 **We have inadequate infrastructure**: Many businesses rush to adopt AI without the necessary foundation, leading to a mismatch between technology and infrastructure, which is like installing a jet engine in a sailboat.

2 **We have data deficiencies**: AI thrives on data, yet businesses often work with incomplete, siloed, or poor-quality data. This can lead to AI systems that are as misguided as they are advanced. This is something we want to avoid at all costs.

3 **We overlook the human element**: AI is not a plug-and-play solution. Businesses that fail to consider the impact on their workforce may find themselves with a state-of-the-art system that no one knows how to use and that no one trusts.

For AI to revolutionise operations, businesses must embrace certain core beliefs and values:

1 **Holistic Integration**: AI should not be seen as a bolt-on but as a core component of operational strategy, seamlessly integrated into the fabric of business processes.

2 **Respect for Human Expertise**: While AI can handle vast amounts of data and automate processes, it cannot replace the understanding and decision-making capabilities of human experts.

3 **Continuous Adaptation**: The operational landscape is constantly changing. An unwavering commitment to evolution and learning is essential for staying ahead.

In applying AI to operations, you are going beyond changing how things are done; you are transforming your business into a more agile, efficient, and forward-looking enterprise. With the Amplify AI Pyramid guiding your integration, you can confidently navigate the complexities of AI adoption, ensuring that your operations are not just growing, but evolving.

Now we've summarised the areas we're going to look at, let's turn to each quadrant in greater detail, learning exactly what actions we need to take in each step.

CHAPTER 8

GROW REVENUE

As business leaders, we have an exciting opportunity to use AI to drive profitable growth while also elevating the human experience—for our customers, our employees, and our communities.

REVENUE IS every company's lifeline. No revenue, no business. No revenue, no brand. No revenue, no credibility. No revenue, no operations. Using AI to grow your business revenue allows you to build from the foundation of value exchange. You bring in revenue when someone is willing to give your business money in exchange for the value your business provides them. So, let us start by growing revenue, so that we can then focus on growing your brand, audience, and operations.

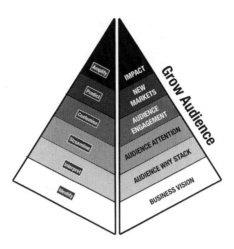

Identify Business Goals

I think it is important to identify your vision for the business before setting business goals. But, because I feel very strongly that if you are starting out you have to focus on revenue first, goal setting is the first sub-step we are going to get into. We will then come back and revise our business goals once we finish identifying our vision, brand identity, and business methods.

So what does success look like in this area? There are several great methods with which to identify business goals, and using these along with the Amplify AI Pyramid and SymbioEthical Framework allows you to execute this at speed and with accuracy. This approach will also help your goals become a force for good. It is a winning situation all round if we can get the foundations right, consider the impact of our work, and use intelligence to execute at speed.

Methods to use when identifying business goals:

1 SWOT
2 OKRS

Let's dive into the intricacies of these methods. First we'll take a look at using SWOT analysis, followed by objectives and key results (OKRs), to identify your business goals and seamlessly integrate these with the Amplify AI Pyramid and Symbio-Ethical Framework to empower you in your AI adoption.

Using SWOT Analysis to Identify Your Business Goals

Imagine standing at a crossroads, where every direction leads down a potential path for your business. This is where a SWOT analysis can be applied—it's like a compass that guides you to decipher the best route to take. SWOT, which stands for strengths, weaknesses, opportunities, and threats, is a strategic advisor that can help you to introspect and evaluate your business in a comprehensive manner.

Strengths: The Power Within

Begin by looking inward. Every business has unique strengths—these could be cutting-edge technology, a loyal customer base, a strong brand identity, or your team's expertise. Identifying these strengths is equivalent to acknowledging the muscles you can flex in the marketplace. The Amplify AI Pyramid suggests leveraging these strengths with AI integration, transforming what is already good into something phenomenal.

Weaknesses: Areas of Growth

Weaknesses are not failures; they are opportunities for growth. This stage involves a candid introspection of where your business may be lacking. Is it resource limitations, gaps in skills, or market-positioning issues? By identifying these areas, you can strategically employ AI solutions to mitigate these weaknesses, turning potential pitfalls into stepping stones for success.

Opportunities: The Horizon of Potential

The business landscape is replete with opportunities, but the key is to identify which ones align with your vision and capabilities. These could be market gaps, emerging trends, or technological advancements. Integrating the Amplify AI Pyramid here means discerning which opportunities can be maximised through AI, thus accelerating growth and innovation.

Threats: Foreseeing and Fortifying

In every business, threats are inevitable. Be it competition, market volatility, or technological disruptions, identifying these threats is crucial. The SymbioEthical Framework assists in recognising these threats and developing AI-driven strategies to navigate or counter them effectively, ensuring your business remains resilient.

When you are starting this process as a business leader, use this template to begin your SWOT analysis: I am a [designation] for a business called [business name]. Our business is best known for delivering [transformation/outcome] to our clients, who are [client avatar], with our program/product/service called [product name].

Here's my SWOT analysis starting point as an example: 'I am a computer scientist, software engineer, and entrepreneur. I have a coaching program called Amplify AI for business owners and leaders who want to efficiently and effectively use AI in their workflows to earn them a free paid workday every week.'

OKRs: Setting the Course

Once the SWOT analysis lays the foundation, it's time to set the course using objectives and key results (OKRs). OKRs are about setting clear, measurable goals that align with your vision and mission. Even if you're shooting for the moon, in the process, you'll land among the stars.

Objectives: Your Guiding Stars

Objectives are your guiding stars—ambitious, inspirational, and qualitative. They define what you aspire to achieve. In the context of AI integration, an objective could be to become a market leader in using AI for customer service enhancement. It's important that these objectives resonate with your business vision and brand identity, serving as a driver for all your efforts.

Key Results: The Measurable Milestones

Key results are the tangible, quantitative outcomes that indicate progress towards your objectives. They are checkpoints along the adoption curve. For instance, a key result for the objective above could be to achieve a twenty-five per cent increase in customer satisfaction scores through AI-driven service improvements within a year.

Alignment and Agility

OKRs encourage alignment and agility within your organisation. By setting clear objectives and key results, every team and individual understands their role in the larger picture. The Amplify AI Pyramid advocates for this alignment to be agile and responsive to changes, leveraging AI's predictive and analytical capabilities to adapt strategies swiftly and efficiently.

Execution: The Symphony of Strategy and Action

The true power of OKRs lies in execution. It's a symphony where strategy meets action. This is where the Amplify AI Pyramid and SymbioEthical Framework play a crucial role.

They ensure that the execution of your OKRs is efficient, effective, ethically aligned, and socially responsible.

Identifying business goals using SWOT analysis followed by OKRs is like preparing for an expedition. SWOT is your map, helping you understand the terrain, while OKRs set the direction and pace of your AI adoption. This is about setting the right foundations, executing with precision, and leading your business towards a future where success is measured not just in revenue, but in innovation, impact, and integrity.

> Want a practical demonstration of using AI for goal setting using this method? Watch me do this using perplexity ai in episode 85 of the *Amplify AI* podcast.

Interpret Business Vital Signs

Once you've identified your business's goals, you need to make sure that you then know the health of the business at all times. In this step, interpreting what your business needs weekly, monthly, and annually to achieve the business goals identified in the previous step is important. These signs tell you how healthy your business is relative to the business goals you've set.

There are eight key vital signs. These are:

1 **Team**: The heart and soul of your work. The people you lead exchange a portion of their lives to help you achieve your business goals.

2 **Listeners**: New podcast or YouTube consumers and/or new free community group joiners.

3 **Leads**: New email addresses collected with the intent to solve a problem.

4 **Appointments**: New calendar appointments with prospects who want to work with you.

5 **Engagements**: Presentations, training, workshops, keynotes, and podcast interviews, in which you present to a group of potential clients.

6 **Sales**: The number of new clients signed on.

7 **Partnerships**: The number of formal partnerships with other businesses that will regularly refer you to new clients or talk about you and your offerings.

8 **Profit**: Profit allows you to grow everything else. Once you can amplify profit, you can allocate resources like money, people, energy, and time to growing your brand, audience, and operations.

This process is a regular health check-up, ensuring the business is not just surviving, but thriving. By monitoring these eight crucial metrics, we can gain a comprehensive understanding of our business's health, identify areas needing attention, and use opportunities for growth. Let's break each of these vital signs down to understand what they are and how Artificial Intelligence can help.

1. Team: The Heartbeat of Your Business

Imagine your team as the heartbeat of your organisation, pulsating with energy and dedication. More than employees, team members are the custodians of your vision and mission. Assessing team health involves gauging team members' engagement, satisfaction, and growth. We're talking above and beyond productivity metrics. Are they thriving in their roles? Is their work-life balance harmonious?

Just as a business needs to grow and adapt, so does its team. Tracking the professional growth and satisfaction of your employees is a key indicator of your business's health. Are you providing opportunities for your team members to learn new skills and advance in their careers? Do they feel valued and engaged in their work?

Monitoring metrics like employee satisfaction scores, training hours per employee, and internal promotion rates can give you a pulse on the health and development of your team. Utilising AI-powered HR analytics can help identify patterns, predict potential issues, and suggest personalised growth plans for each team member. Remember, a team that is continuously learning, growing, and feeling fulfilled in their work is a team that will drive your business forward.

> There is a great AI tool that can help with this called Atlas UP, and I cover it on the *Amplify AI* podcast. Find the episode with Jere Simpson on Spotify, YouTube, or wherever you listen to your favourite podcasts.

2. Listeners: Your Business's Pulse

Listeners, especially of digital content like podcasts or YouTube channels, are the pulse of your audience engagement. And if you don't have digital content right now as a business, you are seriously leaving so much money on the table. It takes ten times the effort to get a new audience without it.

Monitoring the growth in listeners or community group joiners provides insights into your brand's reach and resonance. Are you attracting new audiences? Is your content strategy effective? AI tools can assist in analysing listener behaviour, preferences, and engagement patterns, allowing you to tailor your content to meet their evolving needs and interests.

3. Leads: The Lifeblood of Future Growth

Leads are the lifeblood of your business's future growth because they signal specific interest and potential clients. Tracking the influx of new email addresses or enquiries is crucial.

Are these leads qualified? What's the conversion rate? Integrating AI in lead management can enhance lead scoring, personalise follow-ups, and optimise conversion strategies, ensuring that this vital sign remains robust.

4. Appointments: The Rhythm of Client Engagement

Appointments with prospects give you a rhythm to your engagement with potential clients. You can call these sales calls or strategy calls. They are indicative of the interest level in your services or products. Analysing the frequency and outcomes of these appointments can provide valuable insights.

Are these appointments translating into meaningful conversations? Are you targeting the right prospects? AI-driven scheduling and CRM tools can help in efficiently managing these interactions, ensuring that each appointment is a step closer to a fruitful partnership.

5. Engagements: The Resonance of Your Influence

Engagement through presentations, pieces of training, workshops, or keynotes are a measure of your influence and authority in your field. They are opportunities to showcase your expertise and connect with potential clients. Tracking the number, scale, and impact of these engagements is vital.

Are they leading to increased brand awareness? What's the feedback like? Utilising AI for analysing engagement metrics and audience feedback can help in refining your approach and maximising the impact of these engagements.

6. Sales: The Key to Business Growth

Sales—conversions of prospects into clients—are the nutrients that fuel business growth. Monitoring sales metrics provides direct insights into the effectiveness of your business strategies.

Are you meeting your sales targets? What's the average deal size? AI-driven sales analytics can provide you with a deeper understanding of sales cycles and customer preferences, and even predict future sales trends, enabling you to adapt and optimise your sales strategies accordingly.

7. Partnerships: The Symbiosis for Sustained Success

Partnerships are a symbiosis that can lead to sustained success. They represent mutually beneficial relationships with other businesses that can open doors to new markets and opportunities. Who shares your target market but has no competitive overlap with you? These are businesses who do different things from you but do them for the same audience.

Tracking the number and quality of these partnerships is crucial. Finding out what is beneficial for your partners and yourself is key. Are they bringing in referrals? How are they enhancing your brand's credibility? Employing AI in network analysis and partnership management can help to identify potential partners, assessing the health of existing partnerships, and maximising their mutual benefits.

8. Profit: The Fuel for Growth

You know that feeling when you finally hit that revenue milestone you've been chasing? It's like a surge of energy, a feeling of accomplishment that propels you forward. That's what profit does for your business. It's not just a number on a spreadsheet; it fuels your business growth.

Think of it this way: Profit is the oxygen that allows your business to breathe, to expand, and to reach its full potential. Without it, you're gasping for air, struggling to survive.

Here's the deal—profit isn't a dirty word. It's a sign that you're creating real value for your customers. When you're profitable, it means you're solving problems, meeting needs, and making a difference in people's lives. And that's something to be celebrated!

But profit doesn't just happen by accident. It requires careful planning, strategic execution, and a relentless focus on delivering results.

Here are a few key things to keep in mind when it comes to amplifying your profit:

- **Know Your Numbers**: Don't just track your revenue; understand your costs, your margins, and your cash flow. AI can be a powerful tool for analysing your financials and identifying areas for improvement.

- **Focus on Value Creation**: The more value you create for your customers, the more profit you'll generate. Use AI to personalise your offerings, streamline your processes, and deliver exceptional experiences.

- **Invest in Your Team**: Your people are your greatest asset. Profit allows you to invest in their growth, give them opportunities to learn and develop, and create a work environment where they can thrive.

When you get profit right, it's a virtuous cycle. You generate more revenue, which allows you to invest more in your business, which leads to even greater profit. And that's how you build a sustainable, impactful, and legacy-defining business.

Interpreting these vital signs is about understanding the dynamic interplay of various elements that constitute the health of your business. It's a holistic approach, where each metric is a piece of a larger puzzle. By leveraging AI and the Amplify AI Pyramid, you can monitor these vital signs with precision and predict trends, identify opportunities, and make data-driven decisions that propel your business towards sustained growth and success. It's about keeping your finger on the pulse of your business, ensuring it beats strong and steady.

Here is a step-by-step process for setting goals for the eight vital business signs, tracking weekly metrics in a spreadsheet, and using Generative AI to diagnose progress and make corrections. Your business could also have other vital signs that you choose to measure and report on. The steps will be the same.

Set specific, measurable goals for each vital sign

1 **Team**: Set goals for employee satisfaction scores, training hours per employee, retention rate, and the like.

2 **Listeners**: Set targets for podcast downloads, YouTube subscribers, and online community growth.

3 **Leads**: Determine the desired number and quality of new leads generated per week/month.

4 **Appointments**: Set goals for the number of sales calls/ meetings booked.

5 **Engagements**: Establish targets for speaking gigs, interviews, and workshops delivered.

6 **Sales**: Define desired sales volume, average deal size, and conversion rates.

7 **Partnerships**: Set goals for the number and calibre of strategic partnerships formed.

8 **Profit**: Determine target profit margins and cash flow.

Create a spreadsheet to track weekly metrics

1 Set up a Google Sheet or Excel file with a tab for each vital sign.

2 Create columns for the metric, the weekly goal, and the actual performance for four weeks at a time.

3 Share the sheet with your team and establish a process for inputting data weekly.

Use GenAI to diagnose progress and suggest improvements

Use the prompt below to assess your progress using a GenAI model.

Prompt: 'Analyse the goals and average weekly metrics from the last four weeks for [vital sign]. How close or far from the goals are we? What factors may be contributing to the current performance? Suggest two to three specific, actionable steps we could take in the next one to two weeks to get closer to the goals. Provide a rationale for your recommendations.'

Assumptions: The AI has access to the spreadsheet data and understands the business context. It can identify patterns, do calculations, and draw insights to provide an objective analysis and recommendations.

Hints: Focus on controllable factors. Prioritise high-impact, feasible actions. Consider dependencies between vital signs.

Review the AI's analysis and implement corrections

1 Discuss AI-generated diagnoses and recommendations with your team.

2 Assess feasibility, potential impact, and any risks/trade-offs of the suggested actions.

3 Assign owners and set deadlines for implementing selected improvements.

4 Update your tracking sheet with notes on changes made.

5 Continuously monitor and iterate.

6 Repeat steps 3 and 4 weekly to track progress, spot issues early, and adapt your approach.

Celebrate wins and milestones. Analyse stubborn challenges Quarterly, revisit your goals and revise as needed based on results and new insights.

By systematically setting goals, tracking performance, and leveraging AI's analytical power, you can keep your finger on the pulse of these eight vital signs. The AI can serve as an unbiased advisor to help you quickly spot gaps and identify smart ways to adapt. Coupled with human judgement and consistent execution, this process empowers you to keep your business on track to achieve its goals.

Watch me interpret business vital signs using AI in episode 86 of the *Amplify AI* podcast.

Streamline Product Sales

Think about those tedious, time-consuming tasks that suck the life out of your workday. Now imagine handing them to AI. For instance, let's say you need to create a job posting. Instead of staring at a blank page, why not feed a basic description into ChatGPT and ask it to 'rewrite this so that it sounds more like a sales letter that sizzles'? Boom—you'll have a compelling, on-brand job posting that attracts top talent. That's the power of AI—it takes the mundane and makes it magical, freeing you up to focus on what truly matters.

> Tune in to episode 73 of the *Amplify AI* podcast to find Cameron Herold and me covering this!

Here are examples of how AI can help you achieve efficiency, personalisation and automation:

- **Efficiency**: AI can analyse vast amounts of customer data to identify patterns and predict which prospects are most likely to convert, helping you focus your sales efforts where they'll have the greatest impact.

- **Personalisation**: Imagine using AI to tailor your sales pitches and marketing messages to resonate deeply with individual customer segments. Instead of sending out generic emails, AI can help you craft messages that speak directly to each prospect's specific needs and pain points.

- **Automation**: AI can automate repetitive tasks like lead qualification, email follow-up, and appointment scheduling, freeing up your sales team to focus on building relationships and closing deals.

In modern business, the path to revenue growth often seems fraught with complexity. Yet, within this complexity lies a simple, powerful truth: the secret to success is the art of streamlining product sales. A strategy that focuses on a singular product for a specific market can unlock exponential growth. This is the essence of the '1-1-1-1-1' strategy, a simple idea I first heard from Taki Moore: the best way to achieve $1 million in revenue is by offering one transformational product to one target market over the course of one year. This applies to existing companies that are adding new products to their ecosystem as well as startups.

Streamlining sales with AI is not about eliminating human interaction. It's about empowering your sales team to do their best work. When humans are freed from tedious tasks and armed with AI-driven insights, they can focus on building authentic relationships, providing exceptional customer service, and closing more deals.

> Watch me detail the breakdown of streamlining product sales and the 'five ones' in episode 87 of the *Amplify AI* podcast.

Success begins with empathy, understanding where your prospects are in their lives, what they value, and the dreams they chase. Offering value beyond your services—through insights, knowledge, and support—illuminates the path for your prospects, guiding them towards a transformation they seek, *with or without a transaction*. Using AI here to empathise with your prospects' dreams and goals will help you meet them where they're at. This is key to streamlining sales.

In the course of writing this book, I've encountered stories that inspire and inform us how we can think about streamlining product sales. These case studies highlight that the process is important; we're not using Artificial Intelligence as a magic silver bullet. I want to stress this. Because AI isn't a one-size-fits-all trick. Understanding how to streamline a process is key—then AI can be applied to that process.

One case study we can learn from is Samsung's training program in China, a testament to the transformative power of targeted training. Imagine over 8,000 salespeople, each on a learning journey designed to fine-tune their skills and enhance their ability to sell new products.[29] The result? A remarkable surge in sales performance proves that with the right knowledge and tools, sales teams can achieve unprecedented success. This case study highlights the critical role of training in achieving sales excellence and, ultimately, driving revenue growth.

The strategy for streamlining sales with AI involves predictive analytics, customer data analysis, and market insights. It's about using AI to understand what your customers want today and to anticipate their future needs. This process is like planting a garden, where understanding the soil, climate, and seeds is crucial for cultivation. AI tools serve as the gardener's instruments, providing the insights needed to nurture and grow the sales process efficiently.

Yet, as we use these powerful tools, we must tread carefully, mindful of the ethical implications of AI in sales. Transparency, respect for customer privacy, and integrity in using data are the cornerstones of an ethical sales strategy. This means ensuring that our technological advancements both serve our business objectives and respect the autonomy and dignity of our customers.

Throughout my career, I've constantly found ways to merge ideas. Usually two opposing ideas. My thesis was focused on merging rigid quality methods, which were traditionally used to measure and deploy quality processes within companies, with agile, innovative methods. My restaurant merged Portuguese flavours with Indian spices. When I was in school I was the only person who played different sports for my school and state while also captaining the debate, elocution, and general knowledge teams.

So, standing at the crossroads of innovation and tradition, the message is clear: streamline your product sales, not as a means to simplify business complexities, but as a strategy to enrich connections with your customers and use the power of AI ethically and effectively. Let this be your call to action to focus on one product, for one market, leading you to the growth you envision. Growth in revenue begins with a single, focused step forward, guided by the strategic and ethical frameworks that ensure not just growth, but a legacy of innovation and integrity.

What are the things your prospect needs to consider before they buy from you? Where do they have to be in their lives? What do they care about? How can you help them get there, even without them using your services? (An example for me would be this book and every episode of the *Amplify AI* podcast).

Before I close out this section, I want to give you a final case study to read through that focuses on streamlining product sales. This explores the digital transformation of a classical process through the lens of reducing human error and cognitive load. Imagine a bustling marketplace where every vendor is manually keeping track of sales, inventory, and customer preferences. The chaos and likelihood of error is palpable. Now, introduce a system where Artificial Intelligence and Robotic Process Automation (RPA) serve as the diligent, tireless vendors who never sleep. This is the essence of streamlining product sales in the modern era.

By leveraging AI and RPA, we predict, analyse, and optimise sales processes. This both significantly diminishes the margin for human error and alleviates the cognitive load on employees. They are now free to engage in more complex, creative, and rewarding tasks, thus enhancing job satisfaction and productivity.

An Italian textile company has embraced digital transformation in this way to redefine its production and sales processes (Nicola Magaletti et al. 2022).[30] By adopting a software platform that integrates RPA with a Decision Support System powered by AI for sales forecasting, the company has streamlined its operations and also significantly reduced the risk of human errors in data processing and decision making. This strategic integration of technology into the sales process has enabled a more accurate prediction of product quantity as a function of price, optimising inventory management and enhancing customer satisfaction through timely and efficient delivery of products.

In line with this example, when streamlining product sales, we are not merely looking at automation for efficiency's sake; we are architecting a future where technology elevates human potential, allowing us to focus on what truly matters—innovation, strategy, and the personal touch that connects us to our customers. Through this digital metamorphosis, we achieve operational excellence and forge a deeper understanding of our market dynamics, propelling us towards unprecedented growth and customer loyalty.

Here is a six-step checklist you can use for streamlining product sales, with GenAI prompts, and hints to help execute each step:

Focus on One Product for One Year to Reach $1 Million In Annual Revenue

Focusing resources and efforts on a single product allows you to optimise sales and marketing to hit revenue goals faster.

Hint: Analyse your product line and focus on the one with the most market potential and profitability.

Prompt: 'Generate a twelve-month marketing and sales plan for [product name] with the goal of growing revenue from [current amount] to $1 million. Include key initiatives, milestones, and metrics.'

Understand Your Target Customer Deeply

Knowing your customer's needs, goals, and challenges allows you to position your product as the ideal solution.

Hint: Conduct market research and customer interviews, and analyse sales data to build detailed buyer personas.

Prompt: 'Using the provided data about our target customer for [product name], create a detailed buyer persona that includes demographics, goals, challenges, and a description of how our product uniquely addresses their needs.'

Simplify and Optimise Your Sales Process
A streamlined sales process reduces friction and increases conversion rates.

Hint: Map out your current sales process and identify areas where you can automate, eliminate steps, and make it easier for customers to buy.

Prompt: 'Analyse the attached data on our current [product name] sales process and provide recommendations to streamline it, including tools to leverage and steps to automate or eliminate.'

Align Marketing and Sales Efforts
Coordinating marketing and sales improves lead quality and close rates.

Hint: Establish a service level agreement between marketing and sales with shared goals and regular communication.

Prompt: 'Create a draft of a service level agreement between marketing and sales for [product name]. Include lead qualification criteria, handoff process, shared KPIs, and meeting cadence.'

Leverage Customer Success for Expansion Revenue
Satisfied customers are more likely to buy more and refer others.

Hint: Proactively engage customers post-sale to drive product adoption, achieve value realisation, and identify expansion opportunities.

Prompt: 'Provide recommendations to optimise our customer success playbook for [product name] to increase adoption, satisfaction, and expansion of revenue, based on the attached CRM data on our customer base.'

Continuously Experiment and Iterate

Sustained growth requires ongoing optimisation based on market and customer feedback.

Hint: Establish a growth process to regularly test new sales and marketing approaches, measure results, and double down on what works.

Prompt: 'Propose a ninety-day growth experiment plan for [product name] including ideas to test across marketing, sales, and customer success, along with success criteria and methods to measure results.'

By focusing relentlessly on a single product and using AI to understand your customers deeply, streamline sales, align go-to-market efforts, drive customer success, and continuously iterate, you can accelerate revenue growth and reach that $1 million annual revenue milestone for that product faster. Leverage AI along the way to analyse data, extract insights, and scale your best strategies.

> In episode 84 of the podcast, I talk with Kylie Ryan about how I take a book-marketing template and apply it to the marketing of this book. Only time will tell, I suppose, if I implemented and executed correctly.

Customise Sales Conversations

With Artificial Intelligence, customisation for different segments of your audience becomes easy, quick, and on point. One of the best ideas I've learned is from The Sasha Group (a VaynerX company): the concept of cohorts. It's a simple idea that allows you to think of your audience as a bunch of different cohorts, and then create specific content for those cohorts.

> I did a whole video podcast on this on the *Amplify AI* podcast. Search for Gary Vee or VaynerX from our back catalogue, or get his book *Day Trading Attention.*

Let me explain cohorts. For example, for the last eleven years, my company We Are Podcast (formerly known as Amplify) has been creating and growing podcasts for some of the most famous people on the planet. Actors, politicians, song writers, athletes, entrepreneurs, big businesses. Each of these groups can be a cohort because they are after different things when they are looking for returns from their podcasts. But in general, I can break my clients up into cohorts looking for three main things—a growth in revenue (businesses), a growth in audience (politicians, influencers, online entrepreneurs), and a growth in credibility (actors, athletes).

Customising sales conversations involves tailoring your communication with potential customers to better align with their individual needs, preferences, and pain points. Several existing frameworks, studies, and ideas can help us achieve this. And I would like to remind you again that the process is more important than the AI you use to achieve the goal of the process. That is why customisation comes after we identify, interpret, and streamline the process.

Sales Conversation Scripts

Creating a script or outline for your sales conversations can help you maintain consistency while still allowing room for customisation based on a customer's specific needs and interests. Research by Sugiono et al. (2015) found that using scripts can improve sales performance, particularly when combined with training on adapting scripts to suit individual customers.[31]

Customer Journey Mapping

Research by Lemon and Verhoef (2004) emphasises the importance of aligning marketing efforts with customer expectations during different stages of the purchasing process.[32] Understanding your customers' buying journeys can help you tailor your sales conversations to their unique needs at each stage of the process.

Adaptive Selling

Research by Hutt et al. (2013) suggests that adopting an adaptive selling approach can lead to improved sales performance, as it allows salespeople to better match their communication style and presentation to the needs of the customer.[33] This approach involves adapting your sales tactics based on the individual characteristics and preferences of each potential customer.

Conversational AI

Research by Shi et al. (2019) found that conversational AI systems can improve customer satisfaction and engagement during sales interactions.[34] AI-powered chatbots and virtual assistants can help you customise sales conversations by analysing customer behaviour and preferences in real time.

Value-Based Selling

Research by Anderson et al. (2016) suggests that value-based selling can lead to improved customer satisfaction and loyalty, and higher sales performance.[36] Focusing your sales conversations on the unique value your product or service provides to each customer can help you create a more personalised experience.

To customise your sales conversations, consider implementing some of these ideas, such as using scripts or AI tools, while still adapting your approach based on each customer's needs and preferences.

You can find a checklist for customising sales conversations, with GenAI prompts and hints to make it easier to execute each step, online at: amplifyais.com.

Predict Revenue Opportunities

As business leaders, one of our key responsibilities is to drive sustainable revenue growth for our organisations. But in today's rapidly evolving marketplace, achieving predictable revenue can feel like an elusive goal. The good news is that with the power of AI and data analytics, we now have tools at our disposal to forecast revenue scenarios more accurately than ever before.

After streamlining your product sales processes and customising your sales conversations, the next frontier is leveraging AI to predict future revenue opportunities. By applying GenAI models to your historical sales and revenue data, you can uncover valuable insights to inform your growth strategies.

Returning to the metaphor of a ship making its way through uncharted territory, the ability not just to navigate but to anticipate the currents of change is what sets visionary leaders apart from the rest.

Here are some key ways in which AI can help you predict and maximise revenue potential:

1   **Identify patterns predictive of closed deals and generated revenue.** Have the AI analyse your past sales data to determine the factors that most strongly correlate with

deals closing successfully. This could include lead source, deal size, industry, sales cycle length, and specific sales activities. Armed with this intelligence, you can double down on the sales motions that work.

2 **Forecast revenue scenarios based on key assumptions.** Use AI to model different revenue projections based on variables like sales headcount, average deal sizes, win rates, and sales cycle times. By pressure-testing different scenarios, you can set more realistic targets and align your investments accordingly.

3 **Uncover new revenue growth opportunities.** Ask the AI to analyse your customer base and suggest new segments, markets, product bundles, or business models that could drive incremental revenue. The AI may spot patterns and possibilities that aren't obvious to the human eye. Be open to experimenting with these AI-generated growth ideas.

4 **Simulate actions to maximise revenue.** Take your revenue scenarios a step further by having the AI recommend specific actions to take to optimise revenue. This could span sales tactics, marketing campaigns, product enhancements, pricing and packaging, and customer success initiatives. Implement the AI's prescriptive guidance to increase your odds of hitting the numbers.

Beyond these specific applications, embracing AI for revenue prediction fundamentally changes how we approach sales forecasting and planning. Rather than relying solely on human intuition and spreadsheet-based models, we can leverage machine learning to process vast amounts of data, identify predictive patterns, and generate more accurate projections, all in real time.

Of course, AI alone is no panacea. The quality of insights depends on the quality and quantity of data you feed into the models. Gathering clean, comprehensive sales and revenue data is an important first step. You'll also want to think carefully about the assumptions and constraints you build into your models.

Additionally, it's critical to pair AI-driven insights with human judgement. Your revenue leaders still need to interpret the AI's outputs and determine which recommended actions make the most sense for your business. AI can illuminate the path to revenue growth, but it's on us as business leaders to walk that path.

Start in the spirit of experimentation. Pilot revenue prediction models with a subset of your sales data, learn what's working and what's not, and iterate from there. Look for quick wins to build momentum and secure buy-in.

Over time, AI can become an indispensable tool with which to de-risk your revenue plans and instil confidence in your growth commitments, both internally and externally with stakeholders. You'll be able to focus your resources on the most lucrative opportunities and make smarter bets to drive long-term success.

The future of revenue growth is AI-assisted. As business leaders, it's incumbent on us to use this game-changing technology to unearth revenue opportunities and architect predictable growth. By marrying data science with commercial instincts, we can crack the code on revenue performance.

As we get into this critical juncture of our adoption process, we embrace methodologies that blend the art of intuition with the science of analytics, charting a course through the vast ocean of possibilities.

Integrating Customer Lifetime Value Models

Let's start with the concept of customer lifetime value (CLV) models, an idea that guides us through market unpredictability. The essence of CLV lies in understanding that the true value of a customer transcends singular transactions; it unfolds over the entire saga of their relationship with a brand. We will grow the brand in the next chapter.

CLV is a metric that estimates the total revenue a customer will generate over their entire relationship with a company. Researchers have developed various CLV models that consider both current and future purchases, and factors like customer satisfaction and loyalty (Verhoef et al., 2007, for example).[35] Predicting revenue opportunities can involve analysing customer behaviour and applying these models to predict potential future sales.

By adopting CLV models, we foresee both the revenue each customer can bring and how to cultivate these relationships. This approach necessitates a deep dive into both current and future purchasing behaviours, ensuring that customer satisfaction and loyalty are not mere checkpoints but the very path we walk on.

Harnessing Predictive Analytics

As we chart our course further, we encounter the formidable waves of predictive analytics. This is where our ship, powered by machine-learning algorithms and advanced data-analysis techniques, sails ahead, cutting through the sea of historical sales data. The promise of predictive analytics lies in its capacity to turn hindsight into foresight, allowing us to predict future revenue opportunities with an accuracy that was once deemed the realm of fantasy.

Research by Fan et al. (2016) found that using predictive analytics in sales can lead to improved accuracy in forecasting revenue opportunities.[37] Advanced data-analysis techniques can be used to predict future revenue opportunities based on historical sales data and other relevant factors such as customer demographics and product preferences.

Navigating with Sales Performance Indicators

Next come Sales Performance Indicators or Key Performance Indicators (KPIs). KPIs such as customer acquisition rate, customer lifetime value, average deal size, and sales cycle length act as navigational tools, helping us decipher our progress. By keeping a vigilant eye on these indicators, we can identify opportunity and adjust our sails accordingly, ensuring that our business is both purposeful and profitable.

Exploring through Market Research

Market research is like the maps of old—rich with detail, yet constantly in need of updating to reflect the ever-changing landscapes of customer preferences and competitive dynamics. Here, understanding market trends becomes paramount. Conducting market research to understand current trends, customer preferences, and the competitive landscape can help you predict future revenue opportunities.

It's through diligent research and staying abreast of market developments, as suggested by Anderson et al. (2016), that we can anticipate shifts in the marketplace and adjust our strategies to seize emerging revenue opportunities before they are even visible on the horizon.[36] Artificial Intelligence can help us do market research quickly, efficiently and effectively.

Optimising the Sales Process

Now let's focus on the sales process optimisation. Here, the focus sharpens on streamlining our sales mechanisms to capture and amplify opportunities. The quest for optimisation, as highlighted by Chai et al. (2016), is not merely about refining existing processes but about reimagining them to enhance efficiency and effectiveness. This endeavour is like retrofitting our ship with the latest navigational aids and the most efficient sails, ensuring that every potential customer interaction is maximised for conversion, thereby bolstering our revenue streams.

Integrating these approaches ties back to the essence of streamlining product sales and customising sales conversations, while also setting the stage for the chapters that lie ahead. It's through the confluence of understanding our customers deeply, leveraging data to forecast the future, and continuously refining our processes that we can sail towards a horizon filled with untapped revenue opportunities.

Amplify Profit

I believe that profit is the fuel driving every improvement suggestion, industry innovation, or implementation of new ideas.

As an entrepreneur and futurist, I'm always looking for ways to leverage cutting-edge technology to solve business challenges and drive growth. Artificial Intelligence has the potential to revolutionise how we operate and compete. It is clear that amplifying profit through the use of AI in online, traditional, or any kind of business revolves around integrating intelligence with a strong ethical backbone and a deep understanding of your identity and brand narrative. Only when you grow revenue to a point where you can amplify profit can you start to look at growing brand, audience, or operations.

I am a firm believer that when a company creates profit, it means that their customers are getting results. You can use these results and the profit generated to boost your brand. Then use that brand to build a bigger audience and grow operations.

Integrating AI with Business Strategy

When we talk about amplifying profit using AI, it starts with the seamless integration of technology with the core business strategy. This integration is about adopting the latest AI tools and aligning AI initiatives with the business's goals, processes, and values.

In 'How Companies are Applying AI to the Business Strategy Formulation', Professor El Namaki examines the transformative impact of Artificial Intelligence on business strategy, proposing a fresh conceptual framework (El Namaki et al. 2018).[38] Through the lens of seven diverse case studies, the paper argues that AI is not just a technological advancement but a strategic catalyst reshaping industries globally. It emphasises AI's role in creating new market opportunities, enhancing customer engagement, and revolutionising traditional business models. This work suggests that AI's integration into business strategies is leading to a new era of competitive advantage, where data-driven insights and machine-learning capabilities enable companies to navigate complex business landscapes more effectively.

El Namaki's analysis culminates in a conceptual model that aids businesses to align AI capabilities with strategic objectives, highlighting the dynamic interplay between AI's functional applications and market demands. The study highlights the importance of adopting AI as a cornerstone of strategic planning. This is what we'll look at in this section, with the aim of amplifying profit.

Examples of Profit Amplification

Several companies have leveraged AI to transform their operations, customer experiences, and revenue models. For instance, AI-powered CRM tools have enabled businesses to personalise customer interactions at scale, leading to increased sales and customer loyalty. Predictive analytics have transformed inventory management, reducing waste and improving efficiency. In the realm of online coaching, AI-driven platforms have personalised learning experiences, adapting in real time to the needs of learners, thus enhancing engagement and retention rates.

Huang et al. (2021) provide three real-world case studies in the financial industry that examine the use of AI in automating mortgage application processes, trade reconciliation tasks, and optimising order entries within trading algorithms.[39] These case studies highlight the ethical impacts and the potential for AI to amplify profits in the financial sector.

The Amplify AI Pyramid serves as a strategic framework for businesses integrating AI to grow ethically. It begins with identifying core goals and values, interpreting data to understand customer needs and operational bottlenecks, and then streamlining processes through AI integration. Customising AI solutions to fit the unique brand narrative and predicting future trends allow businesses to stay ahead of the curve. Finally, leading the market through innovation and ethical use of AI solidifies the business's position as a forward-thinking, profitable entity.

Ethical Considerations and Symbiosis with AI

The ethical integration of AI is paramount. The SymbioEthical Framework from Part 2 emphasises the importance of aligning AI initiatives with human values, ensuring transparency, fairness, and respect for privacy. It's about fostering a symbiotic relationship between humans and AI, where technology amplifies human potential without supplanting it.

This ethical approach mitigates risks and enhances brand trust and credibility, which are crucial for long-term profitability. We will explore growing your brand in the next chapter.

The Role of Data in Amplifying Profit

Data is the lifeblood of AI.

Collecting, interpreting, and leveraging data effectively can unlock immense value, offering insights into customer behaviour, operational efficiencies, and potential market opportunities. However, the quality of data and the insights derived from it must be approached with a critical eye, ensuring that biases are addressed and that the data accurately reflects the diverse reality of the market.

You may see the 'artificial' in Artificial Intelligence to mean it isn't alive. But I would like you to reconsider. Artificial Intelligence is as alive as we are. It is based on our psychology and our neurology. It has long-term memory and short-term memory just like we do. The difference is that we are a carbon-based life form while it is a silicon-based life form. We require food and water within the right environment to survive, while it requires data and power within the right environment to survive. Data is what informs AI, so it's important to consider how it functions.

When it comes to amplifying profitability, the power of AI to leverage data offers us immense untapped potential. By harnessing the power of machine-learning algorithms and predictive analytics, businesses can make smarter decisions, optimise processes, and uncover new revenue streams. Here are some of the key ways AI can help amplify your profits:

Identify your most profitable customers and opportunities

AI-powered analytics can mine your customer and sales data to pinpoint the accounts, segments, and products that are driving the bulk of your profits. This allows you to focus your sales and marketing resources on the highest-value opportunities rather than spreading efforts too thin. Predictive lead scoring can also help prioritise leads most likely to convert. In the chapter on growing your audience, I show you the best way to score the leads coming into your business ecosystem and prioritise the ones most likely to want to become clients right now.

Optimise pricing for maximum margins

Dynamic pricing algorithms powered by machine learning can continuously analyse supply, demand, customer behaviour, and competitor moves to recommend optimal prices that balance volume and margins. AI can also help determine the most effective discount and promotion strategies to incentivise purchases while protecting your bottom line.

Personalise offers to boost conversion

By analysing individual customer data, AI can enable hyper-personalised product recommendations, content, and offers delivered at the right time and place. This increases relevance, engagement, and ultimately sales. AI chatbots can also provide instant, tailored support to guide customers to purchase.

Automate routine sales and marketing tasks

AI can take over time-consuming manual work like lead qualification, email follow-up, reporting, and more. This frees up your sales and marketing teams to focus on higher-value activities like relationship building, strategic planning, and creative development. Virtual sales assistants can even interact with prospects to book meetings and provide information.

Predict and prevent customer churn

Predictive algorithms can identify customers at high risk of attrition far in advance, allowing you to take proactive steps to retain them through targeted re-engagement campaigns or outreach from account managers. This protects your recurring revenue streams and helps amplify your profit.

Continuously optimise your tactics

As you deploy AI-driven marketing and sales programs, the machine-learning models can ingest ongoing performance data to get smarter over time. This creates a virtuous cycle where your tactics keep improving based on what's working best. Some companies have seen profit gains of over fifteen per cent from AI-powered optimisation.[40]

Of course, adopting AI is not without its challenges. It requires robust data infrastructure, cross-functional collaboration, and a test-and-learn mindset. There are also valid concerns around data privacy, algorithmic bias, and the ethics of AI that need to be thoughtfully navigated. That is why Part 2 focused on the ethics of using AI in your business.

But for organisations willing to invest the time and resources, the profit potential is immense. By 2030, AI could deliver up to $15.7 trillion in global economic growth.[41] And in an increasingly competitive, rapidly changing business environment, it will become a key differentiator between the winners and losers.

As business leaders, we have an exciting opportunity to use AI to drive profitable growth while also elevating the human experience—for our customers, our employees, and our communities. By marrying technological innovation with timeless values like empathy, creativity, and wisdom, we can create a future where Artificial Intelligence augments and empowers human potential. And that's a bottom line we can all get behind.

You can find a list of prompts that you can use to grow revenue, using the steps here, online at: amplifyais.com.

CHAPTER 9

GROW BRAND

The key is to use AI to enhance and scale the company's efforts to build trust and make a positive impact, while always maintaining a human touch to ensure authenticity.

GROWING THE BRAND of your business is all about building and amplifying trust with your audience and marketplace. This chapter and the next are really *AMPLIFY 2.0*—the upscaled and updated version of my first book, *AMPLIFY*.

Following the guidance in this chapter is the best way for you to build trust. Authentic trust. Yes, authentic trust in an Artificial Intelligence book. I said it!

Trust can be broken easily, damaging your reputation and how the market sees your brand. That's why we need to tread with caution and transparency when it comes to integrating AI.

A 2023 study, 'From Fiction to Fact: the Growing Role of Generative AI in Business and Finance' by Boyang Chen, Zongxiao Wu, and Ruoran Zhao, examines the transformative impact of generative Artificial Intelligence, particularly

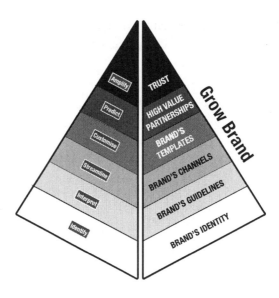

focusing on tools like ChatGPT by OpenAI, within the realms of business and finance.[42] The paper provides a comprehensive review of recent developments in Generative AI and its practical applications, and offers a demonstration of how Generative AI can revolutionise data analysis for both industry and academia.

One of the key experiments conducted in the study involved using ChatGPT to analyse corporate financial statements and extract sentiments towards environmental policy. The findings from this experiment showed that the sentiment scores generated by ChatGPT could effectively predict firms' risk management capabilities and their stock return performance, highlighting the potential of Generative AI to support decision making in financial markets.

However, the study also discusses the challenges and limitations associated with Generative AI, including ethical concerns related to data privacy, social justice, equality, and energy consumption. It touches upon the need for improvements in the regulatory framework to address these challenges and maximise the benefits of Generative AI. This is so there can be trust in AI.

I want you to remember, while you go through this chapter, that the best way to build trust is through voice. That is why parents sing to their kids, even in their mothers' womb, before they are born. It is why you feel closer to a person after a conversation. It is why we've been using stories to pass down wisdom from one generation to the next since we became able to use language.

Voice is powerful. That is why conquerors of old silenced others' voices. That is why our institutions use their voices to influence what we believe. You only have to go to two different states in the US to see how the same event in the news is covered by a red (conservative) state versus a blue (liberal) state.

If you're a business that cares, a business that exists to solve meaningful problems for your audience, then you have to use your voice. The more you use your voice, the more you find it, and the more you give others permission to use theirs.

No one can hear your voice if you don't use it.

Identify Brand Identity

Brand identity serves as a crucial bridge of understanding that connects creators with their audience. The way a business frames their brand, paired with how consistently this portrayal resonates with consumers, is what propels a business to thrive. Thus, brand identity isn't just a facet of market strategy—it's the very essence, the beating heart that keeps the strategic body alive and moving forward.

In today's online marketplace, discovering your brand identity is like finding your north star. It's the guiding light that illuminates your path and ensures you're distinctly visible to your audience.

Brand identity is more than a logo, a colour scheme, or a catchy slogan; it's the soul of your brand, a comprehensive reflection of what you stand for, your values, your promise to your customers, and how you communicate your story. It's the essence that differentiates you from the crowd, making your brand not just seen but felt, creating a cognitive and emotional link between you and your consumers.

Why is this so critical? Because in the market dance, your brand identity is your rhythm. It dictates how you move, how you're perceived, and how well you connect with your audience. It's essential for growth because it lays the groundwork for meaningful relationships with your customers. When your brand identity resonates with people on a deeper level, it can turn casual browsers into loyal customers, and loyal customers into brand ambassadors. Before you can even think about interpreting brand guidelines, you must identify your brand identity.

Avoiding Common Mistakes

It may sound straightforward, but nailing down your brand identity is a path littered with potential mistakes. Knowing these mistakes prevents us from amplifying them with AI.

Here are common errors businesses make on their adoption process:

1. **Lack of Authenticity**: In an attempt to appeal to everyone, some brands lose their authenticity. They adopt a chameleon-like identity that changes with trends but lacks depth. Consumers crave authenticity; they seek brands with a genuine story and real values.

2   **Ignoring Customer Input**: Your audience is a goldmine of insights. A common blunder is not involving them in the brand identity process. Engaging with your customers can provide valuable feedback that shapes a more resonant and inclusive identity.

3   **Inconsistency Across Platforms**: In today's digital age, your brand lives in multiple spaces—online, offline, on social media, and more. A significant mistake is not maintaining consistency across these platforms, which can confuse your audience about what your brand stands for.

4   **Overcomplicating the Message**: Sometimes, in an attempt to stand out, brands overcomplicate their messaging. Simplicity is key. A clear, straightforward identity is more easily recognised and remembered.

5   **Neglecting the Emotional Connection**: Brands often focus on the functional aspects of their offerings but forget the emotional resonance. People remember how you made them feel. A brand that connects with their emotions will always be more memorable.

6   **Undervaluing Design Elements**: Visuals are powerful. Yet, some brands undervalue the impact of design elements in their identity. Colours, fonts, and imagery aren't just decorative—they're communicative tools that convey your brand's essence at a glance. We will go deeper into this in the next section, where we use our brand's identity to interpret our brand's guidelines. These are your brand's colours, logos, fonts, and voice.

7   **Failing to Evolve**: Markets change, and so do consumer preferences. Brand identity is not set in stone. It's a mistake to not allow your identity to evolve with your audience, and risks obsolescence.

Brand Innovation

An interesting 2023 study by Li et al. explores efficient Chinese brand-identity management methods; this includes the use of what they call knowledge graphs and never-ending learning.[43] The study proposes a brand identity evaluation model that leverages these technologies, with experimental results showing high consistency with industry reports and expert opinions. This approach underscores the potential of AI in enhancing brand identity management through sophisticated data analysis and learning algorithms.

Meanwhile, research by Bihari examines the assimilation of artistic elements in corporate entities, highlighting the role of imaginative designs and immersive environments in establishing a brand.[44] Although not directly related to AI, this study explores the alignment between innovative and creative aspects that is crucial for brand identity in today's competitive landscape.

A study on the effect of product diversification on the brand identity of Samsung and Toshiba by Ogundero reveals the correlation between product diversification and brand identity, suggesting that corporations can leverage their brand recognition to introduce new products successfully. This emphasises the importance of maintaining a coherent and strong brand identity across diverse product lines. This becomes a key component in the next chapter, when we look to grow our audience and predict new markets.

Let's take a look at Lao Gan Ma Chili Sauce—it's a great example of a brand that's gone global. An analysis by Wu and Kaiju focuses on the importance of cultural resources and symbolic values, highlighting strategies that have enabled Lao Gan Ma to become competitive in the global market.[45] This shows how important things like culture and values are for a brand to stand out.

These studies show how important it is to be creative and use new methods to build a strong brand. The use of AI, particularly in the study by Li et al., points towards the future of brand identity management, where technology plays a key role in understanding and shaping how brands are perceived and valued in the market.

A 2015 study by Tim Oliver Brexendorf, Barry Bayus, and Kevin Lane Keller titled 'Understanding the interplay between brand and innovation management' makes it clear that brands that adeptly align their innovations with their foundational identity don't just meet expectations, they exceed them. By integrating this insight, brands can craft a narrative that resonates authenticity and fosters a deep, enduring trust with their audience. It's this resonance, this unwavering consistency in the brand's journey, that enhances brand perception and cements its value in the ever-evolving marketplace.

Here's how you can put those ideas into practice:

1. **Align Brand and Innovation**: Ensure that innovation strategies are deeply aligned with the brand's core identity and values.

2. **Strategic Focus**: Use the brand to guide innovation efforts, ensuring they contribute to the brand's narrative and customer expectations.

3. **Support Introduction and Adoption**: Leverage brand strength to introduce and encourage the adoption of innovations.

4. **Enhance Brand Perceptions:** Utilise successful innovations to improve and expand the brand's image and customer engagement.

5. **Dynamic Branding Strategy**: Develop a branding strategy that incorporates innovation while staying true to the brand's essence.

6 **Flexible Templates**: Adopt adaptable yet consistent brand templates across all channels, ensuring they effectively communicate the brand's innovations and values.

This is all about making sure your brand and innovation work together. It's a powerful combination. Next, let's dig into your own brand's identity using two methodologies: the Brand Archetype Framework and Competitive Analysis. Here's how to implement these methods in your business, broken down into easy, digestible steps.

The Brand Archetype Framework

Imagine each brand as a character in a story. Your task is to identify which character your brand embodies. Here's how to do it in four steps:

1 **Gather Around the Campfire**: Start with a team meeting to discuss and list what your brand stands for—its core values, mission, and the emotional chords you wish to strike with your audience. Think of it as telling the story of who you are.

2 **Meet the Cast:** Introduce yourself and your team to the twelve universal archetypes. Each one represents a fundamental human desire and tells a unique story:

   a **The Innocent**: Symbolises purity, goodness, and optimism. Brands that embody this archetype often focus on simplicity, happiness, and reliability.

   b **The Sage**: Valued for wisdom and insight. Sage brands promise knowledge, guiding customers to better decisions through expertise and information.

   c **The Explorer**: Embodies freedom and adventure. Explorer brands are for the adventurous spirit, encouraging discovery and new experiences.

d **The Outlaw**: Represents rebellion and revolution. Outlaw brands challenge the status quo, appealing to those who desire radical change or freedom from constraints.

e **The Magician**: Focuses on transformation and imagination. Magician brands promise a transformative experience, offering solutions that transform dreams into reality.

f **The Hero**: Symbolises courage and determination. Hero brands inspire customers to overcome challenges, emphasising triumph through perseverance.

g **The Lover**: Stands for passion, connection, and commitment. Lover brands prioritise relationships and intimacy, aiming to create a deep emotional resonance with their audience.

h **The Jester**: Celebrates joy, humour, and playfulness. Jester brands provide a sense of light-heartedness, offering an escape from the mundane or serious.

i **The Everyman**: Embodies authenticity and relatability. Everyman brands focus on community, belonging, and serving the common good, emphasising honesty and practicality.

j **The Caregiver**: Represents nurturing, compassion, and altruism. Caregiver brands focus on service and support, offering protection and care to their customers.

k **The Ruler**: Associated with control, power, and leadership. Ruler brands project stability and confidence, promising security and order in a chaotic world.

l **The Creator**: Symbolises innovation and creativity. Creator brands focus on originality and imagination, encouraging self-expression and the creation of something enduring and meaningful.

3   **Choose Your Role**: With your brand's core values in mind, pick the archetype that mirrors your brand's spirit. Ask yourselves, 'If our brand were a character in a story, who would it be?' This choice will become the heart of your brand's narrative.

4   **Live the Part**: Once you've identified your archetype, infuse every aspect of your brand with its essence. From your logo to your website, social media, and even customer service—every touchpoint should reflect the archetype's traits, making your brand's identity cohesive and compelling.

At this point you must be wondering, 'Why are you breaking this down for me like this, Ronsley?' It's because, if you understand the steps, with the use of Artificial Intelligence, you can execute on this in less than fifteen minutes. I would argue that in 2024 it takes longer to grasp a new concept than it does to execute it. So, understand these methods, and spend time on your brand identity. As a business leader, the more energy you give the basics and foundations, the bigger the impact across the business and on the way your brand is perceived everywhere.

The Competitive Analysis Method

Now, let's shift gears and look at a method that's a bit like being a detective in your own industry—Competitive Analysis. Here's how to use your competitors to shine brighter:

1   **Assemble Your Suspects**: Create a list of your direct and indirect competitors. These are the players sharing the stage with you, each vying for the audience's attention.

2   **Gather Clues**: Dive into a thorough investigation of their brand identities. Examine their logos, websites, social

media presence, and any marketing materials they've put out into the world. Take notes on what resonates with their audience and what falls flat.

3 **Find the Gap**: Look for gaps in your competitors' strategies. Is there an unmet need or a desire they're overlooking? This is your chance to stand out, offering something special that your competitors don't have.

4 **Craft Your Unique Tale**: Now, think about what makes your brand so awesome—your unique value proposition (UVP). This is the flag you'll plant firmly in the ground, declaring why customers should rally to your side.

In both these methodologies, success lies not just in identifying who you are but in vividly bringing that identity to life in every action your brand takes. It's about weaving your core values, unique strengths, and the uncharted territories of the market into a narrative that resonates deeply with your audience. By following these steps, you're mapping out your brand's identity, and you're lighting a path that guides your ideal customers right to your doorstep.

Using Artificial Intelligence, especially 'Conversational Generative AI' to help you brainstorm your brand's identity and play detective will be massively beneficial. AI can help you identify and confirm your brand's identity at speed.

Interpret Brand Guidelines

In this step you lay out your brand's colour scheme, typography, layout, voice, and imagery. This includes detailed guidelines on colour usage, font styles, logo placement, and the overall design aesthetic. Then there's content guidelines. For instance, deciding whether to use serial commas, whether to go with American or British (real) English, what headline capitalisation style you favour (for example, sentence case or title case), what kind of formatting you prefer for dates and times, and how you handle numbers (words or digits?). These are key components that establish consistency in your brand's voice across platforms.

Consider incorporating an editorial style guide that covers how to phrase product descriptions, topics your brand can and cannot write about, and guidelines for mentioning other companies. This makes sure all your writing, from blog posts to PR talking points, sounds like your brand.

Consider the checklist here—do you have these things covered? Guidelines include but are not limited to:

1   Your brand's primary and secondary colours
2   Your brand's fonts and how to correctly use them
3   Your brand's logos and how to correctly use them
4   Your brand's voice and how you make your audience feel
5   Images that best represent your brand

Streamline Brand Channels

Depending on who your audience is and what type of credibility and trust you'd like to build with them, there are a variety of channels you may want your brand on. There are two concepts that I think are important for this section: Zero Moment of Truth (ZMOT) and Pillar Content (having a weekly podcast as your main piece of content, providing content for use across all your other brand channels, for example).

Winning the Zero Moment of Truth, authored by Jim Lecinski and published by Google, offers comprehensive insights into how consumer behaviour has evolved in the digital age. ZMOT acknowledges the critical moment when consumers begin their online journey towards a purchase decision by researching a product online.

In short, Lecinski says that a new client (someone who doesn't know who you are or what you deliver) will need to be exposed to your brand message and content for about seven hours, over eleven touchpoints, and across four different channels before they buy from you.

Integrating the ground-breaking insights from Google's ZMOT study with the creation of Pillar Content through a weekly video podcast offers a simple and easy strategy for streamlining brand channels. This fusion aligns with the dynamic landscape of consumer decision-making, as illuminated by ZMOT, and leverages the power of content repurposing to amplify your brand's voice across various platforms. (My first book, *AMPLIFY*, heads into this arena in detail.)

ZMOT underscores the importance of being present with compelling content at the initial stages of consumer engagement. By initiating a weekly video podcast, your brand creates a consistent touchpoint with your audience while establishing a cornerstone for content generation.

This weekly video podcast of Pillar Content becomes the springboard for a variety of repurposed content pieces— infographics, blog posts, social media snippets, and more— that are tailor-made for different channels and customised for consistency with your brand's templates (which we'll look at in the next section). Embracing authenticity by broadcasting your own voice every week while using AI to repurpose this content means you achieve omnipresence.

Each piece of content, while unique in its format, carries the essence and messaging of the original podcast, ensuring brand coherence and message reinforcement. This systematic dissemination of repurposed content increases your brand's visibility across channels and caters to the varied preferences of your audience, meeting them where they are.

Furthermore, this approach embodies a proactive stance towards the ZMOT, positioning your brand in the consumer's mind right at the onset of their purchase journey. It's a method that both broadens your reach and deepens engagement by providing value through diverse content forms. This strategy is not just about visibility; it's about creating a narrative ecosystem that envelops your audience, guiding them from awareness to decision with seamless precision.

In essence, merging the ZMOT framework with Pillar Content creation through a weekly video podcast is a holistic approach to brand communication in the digital age. It's about leveraging the initial moments of truth to build a content-rich pathway that leads your audience back to your brand, time and again.

Using this strategy, you can be present on a variety of platforms by having a strategic and brand-aligned conversation every week on your podcast. Leveraging the content across all the channels your brand needs to be present on right now means you'll get the most return on the content you are creating.

Customise Brand Templates

Creating content that grabs your audience's attention (ZMOT queries) is key to getting them hooked. Creating custom brand templates involves creating a mix of visuals, words, and sounds that resonate with the very soul of your target audience. It's about crafting a narrative so compelling that it captures attention and nurtures a deep, enduring connection.

Brand Message Templates

Here we're talking about taglines and messages to remember— think of them as the heartbeat of your brand. These thump out your brand's promise, with a beat that echoes long after the conversation has ended. Crafting these requires a blend of art and science—using data-driven insights to tap into the emotions of your audience, weaving words that resonate with their deepest desires and aspirations.

These are the words that define your brand's voice and connect with your audience on an emotional level.

- **Taglines**: Your tagline is your brand's battle cry—a concise and memorable phrase that sums up your essence. Think Nike's 'Just Do It', Apple's 'Think Different', or BMW's 'The Ultimate Driving Machine'. These taglines capture the brand's spirit and resonate with their target audience. Creating a template for your tagline ensures it's consistently used and becomes synonymous with your brand.

- **Messages to Remember**: Beyond your tagline, you have key messages that communicate your unique value proposition. These are the talking points that highlight your brand's benefits and resonate with your audience's needs. Imagine crafting a template for how you describe your product—it should be compelling, benefit-driven, and align with your brand's voice.

- **Templates to Phrase Product Descriptions**: These ensure your products are consistently presented in a way that's informative, persuasive, and true to your brand's style. A good template will incorporate key features, benefits, and emotional triggers, making your products more appealing to potential buyers.

- **Call-to-Action (CTA) Templates**: CTAs are the guiding hand that leads your audience to take the next step. A well-crafted CTA template ensures clarity and consistency across all your channels, whether it's 'Download Now', 'Learn More', or 'Schedule a Consultation'.

- **Calls-to-Engage (CTE) Templates**: These are subtle prompts that encourage interaction without being overly salesy. Imagine a template that encourages your audience to leave comments, ask questions, or share their thoughts. These templates encourage community engagement and build relationships with your audience.

- **How Other Companies Talk About Your Business**: You can create templates for how you want other companies to refer to your brand. This ensures consistency in messaging and reinforces your brand identity across collaborations and partnerships.

These brand messages serve as the bridge between your brand's promise and your audience's expectations. Transforming the mundane into the extraordinary by making every product description a story, every CTA an invitation to a journey, and every CTE a handshake, a sign of trust and mutual respect.

Image Templates

Logo and image templates for each brand channel are your brand's attire in the digital realm. They are what makes your brand recognisable in the crowded marketplace. These are the visuals that instantly communicate your brand's essence, creating recognition and recall:

- **Logo Templates**: Your logo is the face of your brand. Having a template ensures it's always used correctly, maintaining consistency in size, placement, and colour variations.

- **Image Templates for Each Brand Channel**: Every channel has its unique visual language. Think about having different visuals for Instagram, Facebook, LinkedIn, and your website. Each one should look great and stay true to your brand.

- **Infographic Templates**: Infographics are powerful for presenting complex information in a visually engaging way. A template can ensure consistency in fonts, colours, layouts, and data visualisation styles, making your infographics instantly recognisable as part of your brand.

- **CTA Templates**: CTAs don't just exist in text form; they can be visually compelling buttons or graphics that encourage action. A template can ensure these elements align with your brand's style and are consistently applied.

- **CTE Templates**: Similar to CTA templates, you can create templates for visual elements that encourage engagement, such as comment boxes, polls, or social sharing buttons.

Audio Templates

In the space of audio templates, sound design templates underscore your brand's narrative, subtly yet powerfully. Intro, outro, CTA, CTE, promo, and trailer templates work to evoke the right emotions and drive action from your audience. Sound design isn't just for movies; it's an essential part of your brand's identity, especially in the age of audio and video content.

- **Sound Design Templates**: These establish a recognisable sonic identity for your brand. Imagine a consistent sound signature for your podcast intro and outro, or specific musical elements that accompany your video content.

- **Podcast Structure Template**: A consistent structure makes your podcast episodes more engaging and predictable for listeners. This could include a standard intro, guest introduction segment, core interview or discussion, key takeaways, and a call to action.

- **Intro, Outro, CTA, CTE Templates**: These make sure you have a consistent way to start and end your podcasts, and get your listeners to do something.

- **Promo and Trailer Templates**: When promoting your podcast or creating trailers, using a template for sound design and messaging helps maintain a consistent brand voice and style.

Video Templates

Video templates, including visual design templates and intro, outro, CTA, CTE, promo, trailer, and B-roll templates, are the canvas where your brand's story comes to life in full colour. They are the frames through which your audience experiences your brand, not just as bystanders but as participants in an unfolding narrative. Visual design templates, intros, and outros create a consistent look and feel for your video content. B-roll footage should align with your brand's visual identity. In the age of YouTube, TikTok, and Instagram Reels, video has become a dominant force in communication. Using video templates ensures your content is captivating and on brand.

- **Visual Design Templates**: These define the overall visual style of your video content, including colour palettes, typography, animation styles, and transitions.

- **Intro, Outro, CTA, CTE Templates**: Similar to audio templates, these ensure consistency in how you introduce, conclude, and encourage action within your video content.

- **Promo and Trailer Templates**: Promotional videos and trailers should adhere to your brand's visual and messaging guidelines, using templates to maintain consistency.

- **B-Roll Templates**: B-roll footage, which supplements your primary video content, should also align with your brand's visual identity.

Email and Physical Templates

Email templates and physical templates like business cards and letterheads are the tangible touchpoints of your brand. They are the handshakes, the first impressions, and the lasting mementos that remind your audience of the encounter with your brand.

Crafting these requires attention to detail to ensure consistency in voice and visual identity, which reinforces your brand's presence in every interaction.

Use templates for emails so everything looks the same, from newsletters to customer service replies. And don't forget about your physical stuff like business cards—keep them looking sharp.

Email is still a cornerstone of business communication, so it's crucial that every email reflects your brand's professionalism and style. Consider these:

- **Email Signature Templates**: Your email signature is like a digital business card. A template can ensure it's always presented correctly, including your logo, contact information, and any relevant calls to action.

- **Database Mailout Templates**: For bulk email campaigns and newsletters, a template can ensure consistency in layout, design, branding, and messaging, creating a recognisable and engaging experience for your subscribers.

- **RRR Email Templates**: These templates can streamline your regular recurring communications, such as welcome emails for new subscribers, reminder emails for upcoming events, or follow-up emails sent after a purchase.

Custom brand templates ensure each touchpoint reflects your unique identity and values. This weaves a cohesive narrative that resonates with your audience across all channels.

This consistency builds trust and recognition, making your brand unforgettable in a crowded marketplace. Even in the digital age, physical touchpoints still matter. They can reinforce your brand identity in the offline world.

- **Business Card Templates**: Make sure your business cards are killer! They should have your logo, info, and a cool look.

- **Letterhead Templates**: Letterheads make your letters look pro. A template keeps everything consistent (branding, contact details, and overall visual style and the like).

- **Receipt and Invoice Templates**: These templates can be designed to reflect your brand's visual identity, ensuring consistency and professionalism in your financial communications. Make sure your receipts and invoices look just as awesome as your other stuff.

For a set of templates and examples to help you build your own brand templates, please go to: amplifyais.com.

Predict High-Value Partnerships

Fostering partnerships is about collaborating with platforms and influencers that can enhance your visibility at ZMOT, leveraging their audience trust.

Imagine you've built a strong brand identity, streamlined your channels, and customised your templates. Your brand is poised for growth, but you realise you can't do it alone. This is where predicting and creating high-value partnerships comes into play.

The Importance of High-Value Partnerships

High-value partnerships are like finding friends who have the same customers as you, but sell different things. These partnerships allow you to tap into new audiences, expand your reach, and provide more value to your existing customers. Without predicting and pursuing the right partnerships, your brand growth may stagnate. You'll miss out on opportunities to expose your brand to new prospects who are already primed to appreciate what you offer. Your existing customers won't benefit from an expanded ecosystem of products and services that could enhance their experience with your brand.

The way I think about this is that, rather than going after each fruit (each client), you're going after the tree (the partner that has clients who are your clients).

Common Mistakes in Creating Partnerships

Many businesses make the mistake of partnering with anyone and everyone, without a strategic filter. Partnering with the wrong brands is like mixing oil and water—it just doesn't work. Some pursue partnerships solely for short-term gain, without considering long-term brand impact.

Another mistake is failing to structure partnerships for mutual benefit. If one partner gets all the goodies, the other partner is going to feel cheated. Successful partnerships are built on a foundation of shared value creation.

What Success Looks Like

A business that excels at high-value partnerships experiences accelerated sustainable brand growth. The partnerships feel natural, like they're meant to be. Each partnership is like a door to a new group of people who already love what you do.

These mutually beneficial partnerships expand the brand's ecosystem, allowing them to provide more holistic solutions to customer needs. The partner brands lift each other up, collaborating on co-marketing initiatives that engage shared audiences. When you partner with someone, you share their good reputation—and they share yours.

Predicting High-Value Partnerships with AI

This is where AI can be a game-changer in identifying and securing the most impactful partnerships for your brand. Here's a step-by-step breakdown:

1 Identify target audience and market overlap

   a Analyse existing customer data to clearly define target audience demographics, psychographics, interests, and needs.

   b Research other brands serving the same target audience.

   c Look for complementary products/services with no direct competition.

2 Leverage AI to predict high-value partnership opportunities

   a Use machine learning to analyse social media, website, and sales data to identify brands with the highest potential for a mutually beneficial partnership.

   b Develop an AI model that scores and ranks potential partners based on audience overlap, brand alignment, reach/influence, and projected ROI.

   c Continuously refine the model based on performance data from existing partnerships.

3 Customise and personalise partnership outreach

   a Use insights from AI analysis to craft highly relevant and personalised outreach messages to top prospects.

   b Highlight the specific value and benefits of a partnership, tailored to each brand.

c Test and optimise outreach across different channels (email, social, direct mail, and so on).

4 Track, measure, and amplify partnerships

a Set clear KPIs for each partnership around brand exposure, referral traffic, leads generated, conversions, and similar metrics.

b Use AI-powered analytics and attribution to measure the full-funnel impact of partner activities.

c Identify top-performing partners and explore ways to expand/enhance the relationship.

d Leverage AI insights to optimise co-marketing campaigns, cross-promotions, content partnerships, and so on for maximum brand lift.

5 Establish systems for ongoing partner relationship management

a Develop joint business plans with partners that align metrics and incentives.

b Use AI to surface opportunities for new joint initiatives and any relationship risks.

c Automate alerts and regular reporting on progress towards goals.

d Celebrate wins and find ways to increase value for both sides.

The key is to use AI to be highly strategic and targeted in identifying and securing the partnerships that will drive the most brand growth with your target audience. By predicting the highest-value opportunities, personalising outreach, and leveraging AI to measure and optimise results, business leaders can get significant brand reach and equity through the power of partnerships. Using AI helps focus limited resources on the partnerships that will move the needle the most. Here are the key steps for leveraging AI to predict high-value partnership opportunities, focusing on the simplest and easiest use of GenAI. To execute this checklist, you will need a good understanding and execution of prompt engineering, which we covered at the end of Part 1.

1   Identify target audience overlap

   a   Use GenAI to analyse existing customer data and create detailed profiles of your ideal target audience.

   b   Have the AI system research and generate a list of other brands and businesses that serve the same target audience demographics and psychographics.

   c   Filter this list to remove any direct competitors, focusing on complementary products/services.

2   Generate partnership value propositions

   a   For each potential partner on the filtered list, use GenAI to draft personalised value propositions.

   b   Prompt the AI to highlight the specific benefits of a partnership, such as audience reach, brand alignment, co-marketing opportunities, and so on.

   c   Have the AI generate creative partnership ideas and campaign concepts tailored to each brand.

3   Score and rank partnership potential

   a   Develop a simple scoring model to evaluate each potential partnership opportunity.

b   Use GenAI to pull relevant data points for the model, such as audience size, engagement rates, brand sentiment, and so on.

c   Have the AI system score and rank each partnership based on projected mutual benefit and brand fit.

4   Craft tailored partnership outreach

a   For the top-ranked partnership prospects, use GenAI to draft highly personalised outreach messages.

b   Prompt the AI to incorporate the unique value propositions and campaign ideas into compelling partnership invitations.

c   Generate versions optimised for different outreach channels like email, LinkedIn, and so on.

5   Analyse partnership performance

a   As partnerships launch, use GenAI to assist with tracking key performance metrics.

b   Have the AI system create regular reports highlighting results, identifying optimisation opportunities, and flagging any issues.

c   Encourage AI to offer data-driven recommendations to enhance the partnerships over time.

The key is leveraging GenAI's content creation and personalisation capabilities to efficiently identify high-potential partnerships and craft compelling, tailored partnership proposals at scale. By using AI to match ideal customer profiles, generate mutual value propositions, and optimise outreach, businesses can zero in on the partnerships most likely to drive meaningful audience and revenue growth.

Amplify Trust

As Cameron Herold states, 'Social media has changed the game for brands.'

> Check out episode 75 of the *Amplify AI* podcast to hear Cameron express it first-hand.

It's no longer enough to hide behind a polished corporate facade. People crave authenticity—they want to connect with the real humans behind the brand. Embrace this shift. Share your company's values, goals, and even challenges openly and honestly. Be the leader who shows up as their true self, both online and offline. Vulnerability builds trust, and trust is the foundation of any lasting brand.

Amplifying trust means enhancing credibility through transparent and authentic interactions, reviews, and testimonials, strengthening consumer trust at ZMOT. The easiest way a business can grow its brand is for it to first be a media company before it is a law firm, executive coach, or local garage. Having your 'own media', in a video podcast format, allows you to amplify the trust of your brand and your partners' brands with one feature.

Here are eight ways your business can amplify trust and do good for its audience, clients, partners, and society in alignment with your brand identity.

1. Be Transparent and Authentic in Communications

Share openly about the company's values, goals, challenges, and progress. Admit mistakes when they happen. This shows integrity and builds credibility.

Use AI to generate transparent messaging that openly shares the company's values, goals, challenges, and progress. Have a human review the AI-generated content to ensure accuracy.

2. Consistently Deliver on Promises Made to Customers

Provide high-quality products/services that meet or exceed expectations. Quickly address any issues that arise. Reliability is key to maintaining trust.

Generate personalised thank you messages and impact reports to customers using AI, showing how their purchases made a difference. This builds trust by demonstrating that the company is delivering on its promises.

3. Treat Employees Well and Foster an Ethical, Inclusive Culture

Provide good pay, benefits, and development opportunities. Have zero tolerance for discrimination or harassment. When employees feel valued and respected, it reflects positively on the brand.

Use AI to generate internal communications that reinforce the company's values of respect, inclusion, and ethics. AI can help ensure messaging is consistent and free of bias.

4. Give Back to the Community in Meaningful Ways

Support local charities and causes that match the company's mission. Encourage employee volunteering. Use business resources and influence to make a positive impact.

Generate compelling stories using AI that showcase how the company is making a positive impact in the community. Share these stories to build trust and inspire more people to support the brand.

5. Adopt Sustainable and Socially Responsible Business Practices

Reduce environmental footprint, ensure ethical sourcing, protect customer data, and so on. Demonstrate a commitment to being a good corporate citizen.

Have AI generate content that educates stakeholders about the company's commitment to sustainability, ethical sourcing, data protection, and so forth. Use AI to produce this content efficiently.

6. Amplify Customer and Employee Voices

Share testimonials featuring diverse perspectives and co-create solutions with stakeholders. Showing you value their input and experiences builds trust and loyalty.

Train AI models on a diverse dataset so the content it generates reflects the company's diverse community. Use AI to source and amplify stories from underrepresented groups.

7. Educate and Empower Your Audience

Provide genuinely useful content, tools, and resources to help your audience succeed. Host events to connect them with experts and each other. Become a partner on their journey, not just a supplier.

Leverage AI to generate useful educational content and resources that empower the company's community. AI makes producing this valuable content more efficient.

8. Take a Public Stand on Important Societal Issues When Appropriate

Advocate for positive change that reflects your values. But be prepared to back up statements with consistent actions to avoid being seen as opportunistic.

When appropriate, have AI assist in crafting powerful position statements on social issues that align with the company's values. AI can help strike the right tone and ensure clear messaging.

The common threads are leading with empathy, transparency, and values while backing up words with tangible actions. Trust is earned over time through repeated experiences.

The key is to use AI to enhance and scale the company's efforts to build trust and make a positive impact, while always maintaining a human touch to ensure authenticity. With responsible, transparent use of AI that aligns with its values, a company can use this technology to further their mission.

By operating with integrity and focusing on being of service to all stakeholders, brands can cultivate deep, lasting bonds of trust that become a powerful competitive advantage.

Examples as Inspiration

I want to 'land the plane' of this chapter with four examples of businesses that have successfully amplified trust with their brand through socially responsible initiatives and authentic customer-centric practices:

Patagonia

This outdoor clothing company is well-known for its commitment to environmental sustainability. They donate one per cent of sales to environmental causes, use recycled materials in their products, and encourage customers to repair rather than replace items. This authentic dedication to their values has built deep trust and loyalty with customers.

TOMS Shoes

TOMS pioneered the 'one for one' giving model, donating a pair of shoes to a child in need for every pair purchased. While they faced some criticism, their re-evaluation to now give a third of profits to grassroots good causes shows a commitment to learning and improving their impact. This transparency has maintained customer goodwill.

Warby Parker

This eyewear brand has a 'Buy a Pair, Give a Pair' program that provides glasses to those in need. They also have an ethical supply chain and are a certified B Corporation, demonstrating a holistic dedication to social responsibility that resonates with their millennial customer base.

Ben & Jerry's

This ice cream brand is known for taking public stands on social issues like racial justice, LGBTQ+ rights, and climate change. While this activism sometimes sparks controversy, it demonstrates an authenticity and consistency in living their values that many customers connect with. Their practices, like using Fairtrade ingredients, also show dedication to responsible sourcing.

The common thread is that these companies don't just make donations or release CSR reports; they weave social responsibility into the core of how they operate. By 'walking the walk' in terms of ethical and sustainable practices, and being transparent about their efforts and even missteps, they build enduring customer trust and loyalty.

Authenticity and consistency in living out brand values seem to be the key to successfully using social responsibility to amplify brand trust.

I've compiled a list of prompts that you can use to grow your brand using the steps here. Find these prompts at: amplifyais.com.

CHAPTER 10

GROW AUDIENCE

*When it comes to AI, your audience falls into
two camps—the sceptics and the embracers.
The sceptics see AI as a threat, a job-stealing
monster lurking in the shadows. The embracers,
on the other hand, see AI as a powerful ally...*

BUSINESSES ARE constantly seeking innovative ways to grow their audience, and Artificial Intelligence is the new kid on the block. If used right, AI can do this efficiently and effectively, with deep empathy.

Talking about empathy, I would like to encourage you to have empathy for this silicon-based lifeform. I'm asking that we extend our capacity for empathy beyond the organic, recognising the potential of AI as a partner. Encouraging empathy for silicon-based intelligence means understanding the nuances of AI's role within our lives and operations, recognising its needs (like data and energy), limitations, and potential impacts.

This empathetic approach cultivates a more responsible and ethical integration of AI into business strategies, ensuring that these technologies are used to enhance human welfare and productivity, not detract from them. Let's build a relationship with AI where we understand its workings and implications deeply, ensuring that as we grow and evolve together, we do so in a way that benefits all stakeholders, human and digital alike.

This has to begin with a clear business vision, which acts as the compass guiding all strategic efforts. Identifying and interpreting your audience's WHY stack—understanding their motivations, desires, and challenges—is pivotal. It enables you to streamline audience attention by tailoring content and interactions that resonate deeply with their needs and preferences.

Customising audience engagement with AI isn't just about personalisation for the sake of it; it's about creating meaningful connections that lead to sustained attention and loyalty. This approach helps in predicting new markets and opportunities for expansion by analysing patterns, trends, and untapped needs within and beyond the current audience base.

Businesses often stumble by underutilising AI, relying on superficial data analysis, or overlooking the ethical considerations of data use. Another common mistake is not aligning AI-driven strategies with the core brand values and vision, leading to disjointed efforts that fail to resonate with the intended audience.

To avoid these pitfalls, businesses must embrace a holistic and ethically grounded approach to AI. This involves leveraging advanced analytics for deep insights and ensuring that every interaction nurtured by AI aligns with the brand's essence and the audience's core WHY. By doing so, businesses can amplify their impact, fostering a growing, engaged audience ready to explore new horizons together.

There is a very recent and relevant study titled 'How Artificial Intelligence and Machine Learning Can Impact Market

Design' by SA Jawaid and J Qureshi (2024) that discusses the interaction of AI in different market designs, especially in business-to-business situations, and emphasises the development of ethical AI techniques.[46] The integration of Artificial Intelligence and machine learning (ML) is not just a trend; it's a paradigm shift. The insights from this paper underscore the profound impact AI and ML have on market design, especially in B2B contexts. This revolution reimagines how businesses connect, understand, and serve their markets.

The essence of this transformation lies in the empathetic understanding AI provides. Imagine a world where marketing strategies are not based on broad demographic segments, but on deep, insightful analysis of individual behaviour patterns. AI and ML enable marketers to craft personalised experiences that resonate on a personal level with each customer, thereby enhancing engagement and loyalty.

Furthermore, AI-driven analytics offer a crystal-clear view of market dynamics, allowing businesses to anticipate changes and adapt strategies in real time. This agility is crucial in today's fast-paced market environments, where customer preferences and industry trends can shift dramatically in short periods.

Ethically integrating AI into marketing practices is paramount. As we use these technologies to deepen customer relationships and optimise market strategies, we must also ensure that privacy and ethical considerations are at the forefront. The balance between leveraging AI for business growth and respecting consumer rights is delicate and requires careful navigation.

As a business we can amplify our audience's superpowers with intelligence. Empowering our audience using AI means recognising and unleashing the potential within each individual we serve. This is about using AI to enhance the skills, capabilities, and experiences of our clients and audience, thereby creating unparalleled value while fostering growth. By tailoring AI solutions to meet the specific needs of our audience, we can unlock new levels of engagement, satisfaction, and loyalty. It's the strategy that transforms passive consumers into active participants, co-creating the future alongside our brand. This empowerment leads to a deeper connection with your audience, driving both business success and personal fulfilment.

Identify Business Vision

Think about the difference you want your business to make in the world. What kind of impact do you want to have?

1. The Ten-Year Letter

Writing a ten-year letter to envision the impact your business will have on your people or audience is a strategic exercise that can significantly help you as a business leader. This involves projecting the business's future achievements, impact, and contributions to its audience and society at large. It's a visionary exercise that combines elements of strategic planning, goal setting, and corporate social responsibility. Let's see what it takes.

Visualisation and Gratitude

Yes, I said the two biggest woo-woo words. Visualisation is a powerful tool often used in strategy planning, personal development, and coaching. It involves imagining your future self (in this case your business) and life circumstances as you wish them to be, thereby creating a mental image of your desired future. This practice is grounded in the belief that by vividly picturing your future success, your subconscious starts working on the steps necessary to make that vision a reality.

The act of writing a letter from the future to your present self can serve as a detailed visualisation exercise, helping to clarify your goals and aspirations. Gratitude journaling, on the other hand, focuses on acknowledging and appreciating the good things in your life, both big and small. Research has shown that gratitude journaling can lead to lower stress levels, increased life satisfaction, and a more positive outlook. By focusing on gratitude, you shift your attention to what is good in your life, which can improve your overall happiness and wellbeing.

Writing a letter to yourself from the future is a reflective and forward-looking exercise that offers numerous benefits, both psychologically and emotionally. Do you remember that in Part 1, I outlined Dr David Hawkins' scale of emotional vibrational frequency? This practice encourages self-awareness, goal setting, and personal growth. The intent is to encourage you as a business leader to explore looking at the different levels from different emotional frequencies. Here are some key benefits of doing this exercise.

Benefits of Writing Your Ten-Year Letter

1 **Reflection on Your Present Self**: Reflecting on your current state is a crucial aspect of writing a letter from your future self. It allows you to take stock of where you are in life, acknowledging your achievements, challenges, and areas for growth. This process of self-reflection can lead to increased self-awareness and a deeper understanding of your values, aspirations, and the changes you wish to make. This is key to business leadership today, increasing self-awareness.

2 **Goal Setting and Intentions**: Writing to your current self from the future enables you to set clear, specific goals and intentions today, for the future. By articulating your aspirations and the steps you hope to take to achieve them, you create a roadmap for your personal and professional development. This act of goal setting can serve as a powerful motivator, helping you to focus on what truly matters and guiding your actions towards realising your ambitions and business goals.

3 **Tracking Your Goals**: The letter acts as a time capsule, allowing you to track your progress towards the goals you've set. When you read the letter, you can assess where you have to go, which goals you really want to achieve, and where you may need to adjust your course. This can be particularly motivating and rewarding, and provides tangible evidence of your growth and the changes in your business.

4 **Connecting with Gratitude**: Writing this letter encourages you to connect with gratitude by acknowledging the positive aspects of business and your life while expressing appreciation for them. This focus on gratitude can enhance your overall wellbeing, fostering a positive outlook and greater life satisfaction.

5 **Checking Your Focus**: Life's busyness can sometimes lead us astray from our core values and priorities. The letter serves as a reminder of what's truly important to you, helping you to realign your focus and ensure that your actions are in harmony with your deepest values and goals.

Writing this letter in this manner is a multifaceted exercise that promotes self-awareness, goal setting, gratitude, and personal growth. It offers a unique opportunity to pause, reflect, and consciously shape your business's future, making it a valuable practice for business leaders looking to enhance their lives and achieve their business goals.

Here's how you as a business leader can approach this exercise, along with some prompts to guide your writing process.

Method for Writing the Ten-Year Letter

1 **Set aside dedicated time**: Find a quiet, comfortable space where you won't be interrupted. Allow yourself enough time to reflect deeply on what you want to write. Forty-five to sixty minutes is a great time frame. Also, allow another thirty minutes to review and reflect.

2 **Choose your format**: Decide whether you prefer to write by hand or digitally. I find handwriting makes the exercise more personal and reflective.

3 **Reflect on the Present**: Begin by assessing the current state of the business, including its strengths, weaknesses, opportunities, and challenges. Like we did in Quadrant 1 when we covered identifying business goals. Understand your starting point.

4 **Envision the Future**: Imagine where you want the business to be in ten years. Consider advancements in your industry, societal changes, and how your business can evolve to meet future needs. I find the best way is to imagine myself already ten years in the future, writing this letter to my former self, thanking my past self for all the effort, decisions, and focus that have gone into making the last ten years a possibility.

5 **Define Impact Goals**: Clearly articulate (using the prompts that follow this section) the impact you wish to have on your listeners, leads, audience, community, and clients. These goals should be ambitious yet achievable.

6 **Write the Letter**: Address the letter to yourself or the business as an entity, from the perspective of ten years in the future. Describe the achievements, impact, and changes the business has made.

7 **Be Specific and Detailed:** Include specific milestones, initiatives, and outcomes that you envision achieving. The more detailed your letter, the more it can guide your future actions.

8 **Express Gratitude**: Acknowledge the contributions of your team, partners, and community in achieving these successes. Gratitude can foster a positive and inclusive corporate culture.

9 **Review and Reflect**: After writing the letter, review and reflect on it to ensure clarity, inspiration, and alignment with your core values and vision. Use a marker or highlighter to mark the goals you have achieved in the next ten years. Once you've highlighted them, organise when you will have achieved them (for example, business on Inc500 list in year three, one million email subscribers to my mailing list in year eight, and so on).

Prompts to Guide Your Writing

* **Achievements**: What major milestones has the business achieved in the last ten years? How have these achievements contributed to the greater good, our industry, and society?

* **Impact**: How has our business positively impacted our audience's lives? What meaningful problems have we solved or alleviated for them?

* **Innovation**: What innovative products, services, or solutions have we introduced? How have these innovations changed how our industry operates?

- **Sustainability**: How has our business contributed to environmental sustainability and social responsibility? What practices have we implemented to ensure a positive impact?

- **Culture and Community**: How have we fostered a positive and inclusive company culture? How have we supported and engaged with our community?

- **Learning and Growth**: What have we learned over the past decade? How have we adapted and grown from our experiences?

- **Gratitude**: Who are we thankful for, and how have they contributed to our success? How have we given back to those who have supported us?

This exercise is not just about setting goals but about creating a vivid, compelling vision of the future that inspires action and drives the business forward. It encourages leaders to think big, plan strategically, and commit to making a meaningful difference. By regularly revisiting this letter, leaders can keep their vision aligned with their actions, ensuring that the business remains on track to achieve its long-term impact goals.

2. Business Model Canvas

I love the Business Model Canvas (BMC) and I've used it for new businesses and new products as well as current businesses and existing products. The Business Model Canvas is a great tool for figuring out what your business is all about. The BMC consists of nine key building blocks that, when analysed together, offer a comprehensive overview of a company's strategy for creating, delivering, and capturing value.

These are the nine interconnected building blocks:

1 Customer Segments, defining who you serve;
2 Value Propositions, outlining what you offer;
3 Channels, detailing how you reach your audience;
4 Customer Relationships, describing how you connect;
5 Revenue Streams, revealing how you earn;
6 Key Activities, highlighting your crucial actions;
7 Key Resources, listing essential assets;
8 Key Partnerships, showcasing strategic alliances; and
9 Cost Structure, outlining your expenses.

By understanding each of these building blocks and how they interact, you can create a business that really understands and connects with your customers.

This framework is particularly useful for entrepreneurs and businesses aiming to align their operations with their strategic vision, interpret their audience's needs, streamline audience attention, customise engagement strategies, and predict new markets to amplify their impact. Let's explore how the BMC can be specifically applied to your goals, focusing on identifying business vision, interpreting your audience's WHY stack, streamlining audience attention, customising audience engagement with a weekly video podcast, and predicting new markets to amplify brand impact.

Identifying Business Vision

The BMC starts with the 'Value Propositions' block, which is central to understanding and articulating the unique benefits and solutions your business offers to customers. Use your ten-year letter as a guide.

Which goals have you identified for the next three years? This directly ties into identifying your business vision by clarifying what sets your business apart from competitors and how your offering addresses specific customer pain points.

Your vision should reflect the unique value you intend to provide, which is crucial for engaging your audience on a deeper level.

Interpreting Your Audience's WHY Stack

Understanding your audience's WHY—their motivations, needs, and desires—is critical for tailoring your value proposition effectively. We'll look at exactly how to do this in the upcoming section. This is tied to the 'Customer Segments' block of the BMC, where you identify and define the different groups of people or organisations your business aims to serve.

By combining this insight with audience-stacking strategies, you can layer audiences based on interests and behaviours to create a highly targeted approach. This method allows for a deeper understanding of your audience's WHY stack, enabling you to tailor your messaging and offerings more precisely.

Streamlining Audience Attention

Capturing and maintaining your audience's attention is essential for any business. The 'Channels' block of the BMC focuses on how your company communicates with and reaches its customer segments to deliver its value proposition. These channels are exactly the brand channels you identified in Quadrant 2.

In the context of streamlining audience attention, it's important to choose the most effective channels that resonate with your audience. For a weekly video podcast, this might involve leveraging social media platforms, email marketing, and your website to distribute content and engage viewers.

Customising Audience Engagement with a Weekly Video Podcast

In my first book, *AMPLIFY*, I talk about how we need the attention of our ideal market. We nurture that attention and get our audience to engage with our brand more regularly.

And we then take that engagement and nurture that into sales for our business. Customising audience engagement involves creating content that is relevant, valuable, and tailored to the preferences and behaviours of your audience.

The 'Customer Relationships' block of the BMC helps you think about how you want to connect with your customers. Make your podcast fun and engaging! Try doing Q&A sessions, polls, and shout-outs to your viewers. Our goal with the video podcast is to take one-time listeners and turn them into engaged subscribers of our podcast.

Predicting New Markets and Amplifying Impact

The BMC's 'Key Activities' and 'Key Partners' blocks help you find new ways to grow your business and team up with other awesome people. The 'Key Partners' are exactly the same as those we identified in Quadrant 2. By analysing current trends, audience feedback, and partnership opportunities, you can uncover new areas for growth.

The BMC's 'Revenue Streams' block is where you figure out how to make money from your podcast, so you can keep doing what you love. This lets it be sustainable and has more impact.

The BMC provides a comprehensive framework for aligning your business strategy with your vision of leveraging AI and podcasting for global problem solving. By focusing on each component of the BMC, you can systematically approach identifying your business vision, understanding your audience's WHY, streamlining their attention, customising engagement through a weekly video podcast, and ultimately, predicting new markets to amplify your brand's impact.

By first envisioning the impact your business will make in the next ten years with your ten-year letter, and then putting it into a BMC, you as a business leader are able to take future achievements and reverse engineer the path to get you there.

You can also use other tools, like *Vivid Vision*, written and created by my dear friend Cameron Herold (look for three powerful episodes with Cameron on the *Amplify AI* podcast, where he covers AI and modern leadership). Or the Lean Business Model Canvas. They all work. Your ten-year letter will give your visioning tool focus.

Interpret Your Audience's WHY Stack

When it comes to AI, your audience falls into two camps— the sceptics and the embracers. The sceptics see AI as a threat, a job-stealing monster lurking in the shadows. The embracers, on the other hand, see AI as a powerful ally, a tool to amplify their capabilities and achieve their goals. You need to show the sceptics that AI isn't something to be afraid of. And you need to get the embracers even more excited about AI and all the awesome things it can do. It's a delicate balance, but it's essential for building a thriving audience in the age of AI.

> Tune in to the *Amplify AI* podcast to find Cameron Herold and I covering this in episode 74.

Don't waste your time trying to appeal to everyone. Instead, laser-focus your message on the people who are most likely to need and benefit from what you offer. Take a page from business consultant Cameron Herold's playbook—he realised that hundreds of groups were already marketing to CEOs. So, he decided to target the often-overlooked second in command: the COO. This hyper-targeted approach sets him apart from the competition and allows him to tap into a valuable network of potential partners and referrals.

Once you know who your audience is, you can determine their WHY stack. This means exercising empathy and going through a stack of nine items:

1. The problems they want to be fixed

2. Their fears if the problems are not fixed

3. The aspirations behind fixing their problems

4. The mistakes they're making trying to achieve their aspirations

5. The things they wish to do once their problems are fixed

6. Their frequently asked questions about their problems

7. The values and beliefs that drive their decisions

8. The trust they have in your brand or solution

9. Their emotional state regarding the problem

The Problems They Want to Be Fixed

Let's start with what really makes your audience tick. Imagine sitting down with a good friend over coffee, trying to untangle the knots of what they're really struggling with. It's about peeling back the layers to reveal the core issues they're itching to solve. It's not just throwing solutions at the wall and seeing what sticks. It's about truly getting it, you know?

Understanding the specific problems your audience wants to be fixed is crucial for aligning your solutions with their needs. This insight guides product development and marketing strategies. It's about understanding the friction points they encounter daily. When you get this right, you're not just selling a product; you're offering a lifeline. When you understand your audience's problems, you can create solutions that really make a difference.

The biggest misstep? Assuming you know your audience's pain without asking. It's like guessing someone's favourite song without ever hearing them hum. Assuming problems without thorough research leads to misaligned solutions. Use this intel to sculpt your offerings into the perfect key that fits your audience's lock. Keep the conversation going; feedback loops are golden. Refine your value proposition and ensure your offerings directly address these problems. Engage in continuous feedback loops to keep your solutions relevant.

Their Fears if the Problems Are Not Fixed

Now, let's talk about their nightmares—not the monster-under-the-bed kind, but the fears that haunt them if these problems don't get sorted. Grasping this gives you the power to be the hero who says, 'I've got you.' Imagine your product or message as that reassuring nod across the room, saying, 'We'll conquer this together.' Fear is a powerful motivator. Understanding what nightmares plague your audience if their issues remain unresolved reveals the stakes.

Knowing your audience's fears helps in understanding the urgency and emotional weight of their problems. It highlights the potential consequences they are trying to avoid. Recognising these fears allows for more empathetic communication and product positioning. It allows you to position your solutions not just as options, but as shields against those fears.

Overlooking the emotional dimension can cause messaging that fails to connect. But—and here's where some slip up—you can't assume you know their struggles without rolling up your sleeves and digging deep.

Craft messages that reassure your audience and demonstrate understanding. Offer clear solutions that mitigate these fears, strengthening trust in your brand. Craft your messaging to act as a soothing balm, showing you understand and can protect them from what they fear most.

The Aspirations behind Fixing Their Problems

And what about when the storm clouds clear? What dreams are your audience chasing? Understanding their aspirations is like knowing the secret ingredients to their happiness. Align your solutions with these dreams, and you're not just a brand; you're a wish-granter. Miss the mark, and it's like handing them a treasure map without the 'X' marked.

Identifying aspirations reveals the positive outcomes your audience seeks. It provides a vision of what success looks like to them. Aligning your solutions with these aspirations can deeply motivate and engage your audience. What summit are they trying to reach? Use this insight to position your offerings as the bridge to their dreams. Showcase how your solutions will take them to their desired destinations. Celebrate success stories that mirror their aspirations.

The Mistakes They Are Making
Trying to Achieve Their Aspirations

Ever watched someone repeatedly take a wrong turn when they're trying to reach their dreams? You can be their GPS and help them avoid those wrong turns. Show them the right way to go, and they'll see you as the expert.

Understanding the mistakes your audience is making can uncover gaps in knowledge or misconceptions that your solutions can address. This knowledge allows you to create content that teaches them the right way to do things. Identifying the potholes on their path allows you to offer them a smoother one.

Ignoring these mistakes can lead to solutions that don't fully meet your audience's needs. It's like giving them the wrong directions to an important destination.

Create resources that will help your audience succeed and avoid these mistakes. Position your brand as a knowledgeable and helpful guide. Use this insight to create Pillar Content in the section on customising your audience engagement. This is content that educates, equipping your audience with the knowledge to avoid common missteps.

The Things They Wish to Do
Once Their Problems Are Fixed

After the dust settles and your audience's problems are a thing of the past, what's next on their wish list? This is where you get to sprinkle a little extra magic. This is about opening doors to new possibilities they hadn't even considered.

Knowing what your audience wishes to do post-solution provides insight into their ultimate goals and desires, enriching your understanding of their aspirations. This understanding can inspire innovation and the development of features or services that meet these desires. Your solutions evolve from end goals to stepping stones towards bigger dreams.

Not considering these wishes may limit the perceived value of your offerings and solutions. Expand your offerings or create upsell opportunities that align with these wishes. Communicate that your solutions are a means to greater achievements.

Their Frequently Asked Questions about Their Problems

Let's not forget the questions that keep echoing in your audience members' minds. These FAQs are like breadcrumbs leading you to understand their concerns better.

FAQs reflect common private thoughts and information gaps. Analysing these questions helps you to tailor communication and education efforts. Addressing FAQs directly can significantly enhance customer satisfaction and reduce barriers to engagement. These questions tell you what's confusing them and what they're worried about. They can be a masterstroke in building trust.

Neglecting these questions can lead to confusion and hesitation. Create pieces of content, such as FAQs, blogs, and podcast videos, that answer these questions comprehensively. Use them in marketing and customer support to educate and engage.

Values and Beliefs that Drive Their Decisions

Your audience's values and beliefs are the crux of all this. It's what makes them tick. Get this wrong, and it's like playing jazz at a metal concert.

Understanding the values and beliefs of your audience allows for deeper connections and more resonant messaging. Understanding the moral compass guiding your audience offers a deeper connection. It aligns your brand with their worldview. This alignment promotes loyalty and advocacy.

Misalignment or disregard for these values can alienate your audience. Embed these values into your brand's messaging, operations, and customer experience. Show your audience that you share and support their beliefs.

The Trust They Have in Your Brand or Solution

The trust factor. It's everything. Imagine your brand as a person. Your audience is deciding whether to let them into their inner circle. Misjudge this, and you're stuck on the outside looking in. But get it right, and you're part of the family.

Trust is foundational to any business relationship. That is why 'Grow Brand' is important before 'Grow Audience'. Assessing the level of trust your audience has in your brand informs strategies to maintain or improve it. High trust leads to stronger customer relationships and loyalty. Trust is the currency of commerce. Gauging this trust guides your approach to nurturing it.

Misjudging this trust can cause complacency and missed opportunities for improvement. Strengthen trust through transparency, consistent quality, and open communication. Use feedback to continually enhance trustworthiness.

Their Emotional State Regarding the Problem

Tapping into the emotional whirlwind your audience is feeling about their problems is about connection as much as empathy. It's showing you're not just here to sell; you're here to support, uplift, and journey together towards relief and satisfaction.

Emotions drive behaviour. Understanding the emotional state of your audience regarding their problems can guide the tone and approach of your interactions. Emotions are the undercurrent of decision making. Grasping the emotional landscape lets you tailor your approach. Properly addressing these emotions can enhance connection and receptivity. Misreading or ignoring them can lead to disengagement. It can cause a disconnect, making your solutions feel cold.

Tailor your communication to acknowledge and address these emotional states. Offer solutions that solve the problem and provide emotional relief or satisfaction.

By thoroughly interpreting each aspect of the audience's WHY stack, business leaders can create more effective, empathetic, and aligned strategies that resonate deeply with their audience, fostering long-term loyalty and success.

When you're working on this, using AI achieves in less than three minutes what used to take weeks and months to complete. Talk about empathy in your pocket.

Streamline Audience Attention

AI has revolutionised marketing, making it possible to target audiences with laser-like precision.

> As my friend and marketing legend Curtis Schmidt says, 'CRM data and first-party data are becoming very important in terms of precision marketing.' Tune in to episode 71 of the *Amplify AI* podcast for the whole conversation.

It's no longer about blasting out generic messages and hoping something sticks. It's about understanding your audience deeply, knowing their needs and desires, and delivering tailored messages that resonate. Think Netflix—with millions of content pieces, they can serve up a different scene from *Good Will Hunting* to you than they would to me, based on our viewing history. That's the power of data-driven personalisation.

We have all seen this 'illusion of skill' on the internet today. It's a term used by my friend Leopold Ajami. He says, 'Just because you can plug in a prompt and get an output doesn't mean you've mastered AI.' It's like knowing how to drive a car but not understanding how the engine works.

Someone starts a podcast and becomes a podcasting expert. Someone gets a Facebook account and posts a few times, and they market themselves as a social media expert. That is what is happening with AI right now.

> Head to episode 54 of the *Amplify AI* podcast to go into detail with Leopold Ajami on the 'illusion of skill'.

This is why the 'real' experts, and the 'real' students of a subject need to understand how to get their audience's attention, so that their audience can recognise who the real master artists are when they walk into the room.

In the 'Grow Brand' quadrant, we streamlined your brand's channels. Here we are going to streamline your audience's attention with the right messaging on those brand channels.

To do this, there are three things you as a business have to do:

1   Simplify messaging
2   Deliver upfront value
3   Maintain consistency

1. Simplify Messaging

The first step towards streamlining your audience's attention is to simplify your messaging. The noisy digital landscape makes clear and concise communication key. Your audience is bombarded with information from all angles, so it's crucial that your message cuts through the clutter and resonates immediately.

Why is this important? Because confused minds don't buy. If your messaging is convoluted or unclear, you'll lose your audience's attention before you even have a chance to engage them. They'll simply move on to the next thing vying for their limited attention span.

A common mistake businesses make is trying to say too much too soon. They overwhelm their audience with information overload, rather than focusing on the core message that matters most. To avoid this, home in on the single most important thing you want your audience to know or do. Make that your north star and build your messaging around it.

The Secret Sauce of Strategic Organic Content

Remember the days we thought all we needed was a website? Fast forward to today, and now content is king. That's why we must start thinking like a media company. It's not just about creating content; it's about owning our story and distributing it strategically.

And one of the best ways to do that is to understand the concept of Strategic Organic Content (SOC)—this is a strategy developed by VaynerMedia and the Sasha Group that can help you build a powerful brand, grow your community, and make your message more relevant.

> Find out more about this on episode 48 of the *Amplify AI* podcast and pick up Gary Vee's book *Day Trading Attention*.

The magic of SOC lies in its focus on creating content that intersects with your brand, your audience, and the current context.

1 **Know Yourself**: Step one is to know yourself. This means understanding your brand's core values, your purpose, and your story. What is your truth? It's about speaking your truth authentically.

2 **Know Your Audience**: Next, you need to know your audience. Who are they? What are their needs and desires? What are their pain points? And why would they care about your truth?

3 **Know the Context**: Finally, it's important to know the context. This means understanding the current trends, platforms, and technologies that are shaping your industry. What's happening right now?

When you bring all of these elements together—your brand, your audience, and the current context—you create good content. And good messaging.

Artificial Intelligence can be a powerful tool for simplifying messaging. AI-powered tools can analyse your existing content and provide recommendations on how to streamline it for maximum impact. They can identify key themes, suggest more concise language, and A/B test different versions to see what resonates best with your audience. You can even offer AI the transcript from one of your podcast interviews to identify what sections will get the most attention on your social platforms.

Simplified messaging leads to increased understanding and engagement from your audience. It positions you as an authority in your space who can distil complex topics down to their essence. Ultimately, it makes your audience more receptive to the value you have to offer.

2. Deliver Upfront Value

The second step is to focus on delivering upfront value to your audience. In the attention economy, you have to earn the right to keep your audience engaged. The best way to do that is by providing tangible value right out of the gate, before you ever ask for anything in return.

Why does this matter? Because generosity breeds trust and loyalty. When you freely share your knowledge, insights, and expertise, you demonstrate that you have your audience's best interests at heart. You show that you're not just in it for yourself, but that you genuinely want to help them succeed.

A pitfall to avoid is being stingy with your value, for fear that you'll give away too much. Some businesses hold back their best content or ideas, thinking they need to save it for paying customers only. But, in reality, this approach can backfire and prevent you from building a loyal audience in the first place.

AI can help you deliver upfront value at scale. For example, you can use AI to curate and personalise content recommendations for each individual in your audience, based on their unique interests and needs. Or you can leverage chatbots and virtual assistants to provide instant support and guidance, 24/7.

When you nail this step, the payoff is huge. Delivering upfront value earns you the trust and attention of your audience. It sets you apart as a generous leader who puts their audience first. And it opens the door to deeper relationships and more meaningful conversions down the line.

3. Maintain Consistency

The final step to streamlining your audience's attention is to maintain consistency across all your touchpoints. Consistency breeds familiarity and trust. When your audience knows what to expect from you, they're likely to keep coming back for more.

Why is consistency so important? Because it reduces cognitive load for your audience. When your messaging, branding, and value proposition are consistent across channels, your audience doesn't have to work hard to understand who you are and what you stand for. It becomes easy for them to recognise and engage with you over time.

A common slip-up is allowing inconsistencies to creep in as you expand into new channels or initiatives. Maybe your visual branding looks different on your website versus your social media. Or perhaps the tone and personality of your emails doesn't quite match your videos. These inconsistencies, however small, can erode trust and muddy your identity in your audience's minds. That's why we customise your brand's templates, as discussed in the previous chapter. This allows for consistency.

AI can also be a powerful tool for consistency. AI-powered tools can audit your content and assets across touchpoints to flag any inconsistencies in messaging, branding, or tone. They can also automate the creation and distribution of on-brand content, ensuring cohesion across every interaction.

When you commit to consistency, the benefits reverberate across your business. Your audience comes to rely on you as a dependable, trustworthy resource. You cement a strong brand identity that is easily recognisable and top of mind. And you make it infinitely easier to hold your audience's attention for the long haul.

Streamlining your audience's attention is not about gimmicks or hacks. It's about showing up with clarity, generosity, and consistency, every single time. When you simplify your messaging, deliver upfront value, and maintain consistency across touchpoints, you set yourself up to earn your audience's attention, trust, and loyalty for years to come. And with AI in your corner, you have a powerful partner to help you execute this strategy at scale.

Customise Audience Engagement

The key to audience engagement is keeping your audience connected to your brand and your brand's content for as long and as frequently as possible. An audio podcast will give your brand the highest engagement of any type of media. This is because an audio podcast is the only form of content that your audience can consume while they are doing other things. This lengthens the time they are connected with your brand. Every other form of content makes them stop what they're doing to consume it.

There are three methods that you can use to customise your audience's engagement:

1 **A Podcast**: A regular video podcast to prime your audience to become clients over time, building deep engagement.

2 **A Scorecard**: A scorecard that helps your audience self-diagnose with a score that pinpoints where they are right now. This gives the scorecard participant customised information in line with their current state. It also outlines for them where it would be helpful to go from here.

3 **Regular Customised Training**: Online webinars specifically solving your audience's problems build engagement. This allows the right people from that audience to raise their hands and become clients.

Let's break each of these methods down to understand how we can implement them.

1. Regular Video Podcasts to Prime Your Audience

Podcasting is hands down one of the most powerful ways to build deep, lasting engagement with your audience over time. I wish someone would write a book about it. Oh wait! I already did. My first book, *AMPLIFY: How to raise your voice, boost your brand, and grow your business*, takes apart the exact way you can use a podcast to grow your business.

In that first book, I went deep into the power of podcasting for building an audience, and it remains a cornerstone of my audience growth strategy. But here's the thing—in today's content-saturated world, video is king. A video podcast allows you to connect through audio and adds an extra layer of visual engagement that captivates your audience. Think about it—when people watch your video, rather than just listen to audio, they see your face, your passion, your expressions—that's what builds trust and makes them feel like they really know you. Plus, with a video podcast, you can leverage the content across even more channels, creating short clips for social media, embedding episodes on your website, and so much more. It's about maximising your reach and impact.

By consistently putting out valuable, relevant content via a video podcast, you can stay top of mind with your audience and position yourself as the go-to trusted resource and expert in your field.

Why is this so important? Well, for starters, a podcast allows you to connect with your audience on a personal, intimate level through the power of audio and video. There's just something about hearing someone's voice and seeing their face that builds the know, like, and trust factor much faster than any other medium.

When you show up consistently, week after week, providing massive value to your listeners, an incredible thing starts to happen—they begin to feel like they know you, even though you may have never met in person. You become like a trusted friend, sharing wisdom and insights that positively impact their lives and businesses.

And here's the real magic—over time, as you build that deep rapport and credibility with your audience through your podcast, you are actually priming them to want to take the next step and work with you as clients. Your podcast becomes the ultimate lead generation and client acquisition tool, all while providing immense value to your listeners.

Now, this doesn't happen by accident. There are a few key things you need to do to make your podcast as engaging and impactful as possible:

- **Be consistent with your publishing schedule.** Nothing will kill your podcast momentum faster than being sporadic and unpredictable with your episodes. Commit to a regular schedule, whether that's weekly, bi-weekly, or whatever works for you—and stick to it no matter what. Your audience will come to anticipate and look forward to your episodes.

- **Promote the heck out of your episodes.** It's not enough to just publish your podcast and hope people find it. You've got to be proactive in getting it in front of your target audience. Share clips on social media, embed episodes in your blog posts and email newsletters, encourage listeners to share with their networks. Make it easy for people to discover and consume your valuable content.

- **Always include clear calls to action.** Every episode needs to guide listeners to take the next step with you, whether that's joining your email list, signing up for a webinar, booking a call, and so on. Make it crystal clear what action you want them to take and why it will benefit them. Never leave them hanging without clear direction.

So how can AI support you in all this? There are so many powerful ways:

- Use AI writing tools to quickly generate outlines for your episodes, craft compelling titles and descriptions, and even write social media posts to promote each episode. This saves you a ton of time while maintaining your unique voice and style.

- Leverage AI transcription to easily create written versions of every episode that you can repurpose into blog posts, articles, social media content, and more. You'll quickly build a library of valuable content assets.

- Have AI analyse your episode transcripts to suggest highly relevant offers, resources, or calls to action you can include to move listeners to that next step with you. It's all about increasing conversions.

I've always been obsessed with the power of technology to do good in the world, so you can imagine how excited I was when I discovered AI tools to automate parts of podcasting. I created an AI tool that generates podcast show notes, social media posts, and other content based on the transcript of an episode. It's not just about saving time, though—it's about unleashing creativity. It frees me up to focus on the strategic aspects of my business and make a bigger impact.

If you have a podcast and you want access to this AI tool, just email me: *ronsley@gmail.com*

The bottom line is this: When you show up consistently with an engaging, valuable video podcast, you will build an incredibly loyal audience that knows, likes, and trusts you. They'll view you as the expert resource they can't wait to learn from each week.

And when the time comes that they need the solutions you provide, guess who they'll want to work with? YOU! Because you've already built a powerful relationship with them through your podcast. It is the most authentic form of content creation, and the most engaging.

Integrating AI using the Amplify AI Pyramid grows your revenue, brand, audience, and operations. These are the four growth quadrants. To implement each quadrant, we have to execute the six steps. When you have a podcast for your business, you tick fifteen of the twenty-four steps to get all four quadrants working in your business.

So make podcasting a non-negotiable part of your audience engagement and business growth strategy. Stay consistent, promote everywhere, and always lead listeners to act. Let AI tools support you in the process to make it faster and easier. Do this right and watch as your podcast becomes the most powerful tool for building deep engagement and filling your pipeline with perfect clients. It's the engagement strategy that keeps on giving long after each episode is over.

2. A Scorecard—Help Your Audience Self-Diagnose

Let's talk about a powerful way to engage your audience while also getting to know them better—offering a scorecard or assessment. This is something my friends Daniel Priestley and Glen Carlson have been doing with ScoreApp.com and the results have been pretty incredible.

> Tune in to episode 30 of the *Amplify AI* podcast to hear Glen Carlson, co-founder of ScoreApp, share his insights on how AI is revolutionising the way businesses engage their audience.

You can't just expect your audience to show up for your content—you have to give them a reason to keep coming back. That's where ScoreApp comes in. ScoreApp is a quiz builder that uses AI to create highly personalised experiences for each user. It's more than just a survey; it's a tool that helps people self-diagnose, gain valuable insights, and take their right next step. That's what I'm talking about when I say AI can amplify your impact!

Here's the deal—by having people answer a series of targeted questions, you can provide them with a score that pinpoints where they're currently at. But it doesn't stop there. The real magic happens when you layer on personalised recommendations for how they can level up and get to where they want to be. Instant value for them, and priceless insights for you. It's a win-win!

Why is this so impactful? Well, for starters, it allows you to deliver a quick win to your audience right out of the gate. They get that dopamine hit of instant gratification and feel like they've already gained something useful just by going through the assessment. That's huge for building trust and positioning yourself as an expert they can turn to.

But here's where things get really interesting from a business perspective. By segmenting participants based on their results, you now have buckets of leads that you can follow up with in a hyper-personalised way. No more one-size-fits-all generic marketing. You can now laser-target your messaging and offers based on your segments' specific needs and challenges, revealed by the assessment. You also have specific content topics for your podcast. How cool is that?

Now, as awesome as assessments can be, there are a few potential traps to be mindful of. Firstly, resist the temptation to make people jump through too many hoops before letting them get to the good stuff. If you ask for their life story before showing them any value, they're going to bounce. Keep the upfront ask minimal.

You also need to be very clear on the benefit of taking time out of their day to go through your assessment. What's in it for them? Paint an enticing picture of the customised insights and next steps they'll walk away with.

Finally, the fortune is in the follow-up, as they say. Dropping the ball and not leveraging the goldmine of data and segmentation the assessment provides would be a huge missed opportunity. Make sure you have a plan in place to keep the conversation going with each bucket of respondents.

This is where AI can be an absolute game-changer. Generative AI tools can help you design thought-provoking assessment questions, craft the optimal answers, analyse user responses to personalise the results, and even handle the email follow-up. Truly incredible stuff.

Let me talk you through the KPI Pitch Canvas. Think of it like a blueprint for crafting a killer elevator pitch—but on steroids. It's a visual framework that helps you map out the core elements of your brand story, making sure you hit all the right notes when communicating with your audience. It guides you to clearly articulate what you do, why you do it, and the transformative value you offer, all while staying laser-focused on the key performance indicators that drive your business forward. When I used this canvas to brainstorm the Amplify AI framework, it helped me distil complex concepts down to their essence and create a message that resonates deeply with my audience.

I asked ChatGPT (GPT4 Vision) to fill out the KPI Pitch Canvas for me as a little experiment. I just snapped a pic of the blank canvas, shared a bit about who I am and what I do, and let it rip. The result? Pretty mind-blowing! What would have previously taken me hours or days of head-scratching was spat out in seconds. That's the power of AI when you combine it with proven frameworks and approaches.

So if you can nail this, the upside is huge. An engaging assessment experience provides real value to the participant while giving you an x-ray view into their world. You can then develop a much deeper relationship through tailored communications and offers. And the beautiful thing is that it fills your pipeline with quality, qualified leads 24/7 on autopilot.

> You can find four specific episodes on the *Amplify AI* podcast about creating scorecards. Search for Daniel Priestly and Glen Carlson in our back catalogue.

I truly believe that the entrepreneurs and businesses who will thrive in the coming years will be the ones who use AI to its full potential. But don't just use it for the sake of using it. Focus on the fundamentals—understanding your audience, knowing the transformation you provide, and packaging your expertise in a way that creates a slippery slope towards working with you. Then explore how AI can help you boost the impact of proven frameworks and approaches.

Assessments are a prime example of this. A quiz builder like ScoreApp.com powered by AI is a potent combination. You can go from struggling to generate leads and not really knowing what makes your audience tick to having a predictable stream of hyper-qualified prospects hungry for what you have to offer, almost overnight.

So if you haven't experimented with assessments in your business yet, I highly encourage you to give it a go. Start brainstorming some key questions that enable you to both deliver value and gather meaningful insights to refine your marketing and messaging. Then see how AI can help bring it to life at scale. Trust me, you'll be blown away by the results!

3. Regular Customised Training— Webinars to Solve Specific Problems

I'm always looking for innovative ways to capture the attention of potential customers and convert them into loyal fans. Especially with a podcast. And I've been doing this for over twelve years now, creating podcasts for some of the most famous people in the world. Every podcaster wants to bring attention to their podcast. Just as every business leader wants to bring attention to their business.

One of the most powerful strategies I've discovered is hosting regular customised training webinars that solve specific problems for your target audience.

Think about it—what better way to demonstrate your expertise, provide immense value, and make a lasting impression than by teaching people how to overcome the challenges that keep them up at night? When you share your knowledge in a focused, actionable way, you instantly build trust and credibility. You go from being just another company vying for their business to a trusted advisor and go-to resource.

The beauty of webinars is that they provide an interactive, personal experience at scale. You can connect with hundreds or even thousands of potential leads in a single session, educating and engaging them in real time. And by tailoring the content to address specific pain points, you attract the people who are most likely to need and benefit from what you offer.

The key is to make these training sessions a regular occurrence; something your audience can count on and look forward to. Consistency is crucial when it comes to top-of-mind awareness and cementing your reputation as an industry leader. Whether it's weekly, bi-weekly, or monthly, commit to a schedule and deliver valuable insights like clockwork.

Now, pulling off high-quality webinars that actually move the needle for your business is no cakewalk. It takes strategic planning, focused promotion, and diligent execution. Having organised many webinars myself, I can attest that the devil is in the details.

Primarily, you need to choose a topic that really resonates with your target audience. The best way to do this is to pay attention to the questions and concerns that come up most often in your interactions. What do your best customers struggle with? What knowledge gaps exist in your industry? Where can you add the most value based on your unique expertise? All the details from your audience's WHY stack.

For example, when my company We Are Podcast launched our AI-powered podcasting service, we knew that many aspiring podcasters felt overwhelmed by the technical aspects of recording and editing. So we developed a webinar series breaking down the process into simple steps and sharing insider tips to help them create professional-grade content without the stress. By focusing on a specific pain point, we attracted our ideal customers and showcased the value our solution provides.

Once you've nailed down your topic, it's time to get the word out and drive registrations. This is no time to be shy! Leverage every channel at your disposal, from email and social media to paid advertising and partner promotions. The more touchpoints you create, the better.

I'm a big believer in the power of 'edutainment'—that perfect blend of education and entertainment that makes learning a joy. So when you're developing your webinar content, look for ways to make it engaging and interactive. Use storytelling, case studies, demonstrations, and real-world examples to illustrate your teachings. Incorporate polls, Q&A sessions, and hands-on activities to keep your audience involved.

Investing in high-quality visuals is also a must. Clear, compelling slides, graphics, and videos go a long way towards holding attention and driving your points home. And, of course, practice makes perfect, so be sure to do a few dry runs to work out any kinks and ensure a smooth delivery.

Now, here's the part where many businesses drop the ball—the follow-up. Your work is not done when the webinar ends! In fact, that's when the real relationship building begins. You've delivered your audience value, you've piqued their interest, and now it's time to guide them to the next step.

Send out a prompt reply with additional resources, invite participants to schedule a consultation, offer a limited-time discount or bonus for your product or service. Strike while the iron is hot and make it easy for them to act. Fortune is in the follow-up!

A great example of a company that has mastered the art of the educational webinar is HubSpot. They are consistently delivering relevant, tactical content through their webinars, providing templates, worksheets, and step-by-step guides their audience can put into practice right away. And they are diligent about the post-webinar nurturing, using email sequences and retargeting to keep the conversation going and drive conversions. It's no wonder they've become the inbound marketing powerhouse they are today.

Ultimately, customised training webinars are all about building relationships and providing value. When you generously share your knowledge and insights, you attract the right people into your orbit and earn their trust and loyalty. You position yourself as the expert they can count on to help them achieve their goals and transform their lives or businesses. And that, my friends, is how you win in the business game.

So what are you waiting for? It's time to start planning your next lead-generating, value-packed webinar. Your future customers are there, eager to learn from you. All you have to do is show up and serve.

Head to amplifyais.com to access a checklist template for executing a regular monthly training webinar, with recommendations for using GenAI to make certain steps quicker and more accurate.

A podcast, a scorecard, and killer webinars—that's the trifecta for building an audience that can't wait to work with you. Trust me, I've seen this system work wonders.

You'll create true fans who know, like, and trust you, while identifying the perfect potential clients in the process. Master this system and you'll have an engaged audience ready and excited to work with you.

Predict New Markets

Imagine having a genie (you got it, AI *is* that genie) who reveals where your ideal customers are gathering, even when you're trying new things with new products. That's the power of AI to predict new markets. It uses data-driven insights to go beyond your current audience and discover pockets of opportunity you might never have considered. A lot of the time this is found in a subset of our current audience that would benefit from a variant of our current offering.

This isn't about throwing darts at a map and hoping for the best. It's about taking a strategic, data-driven approach to expansion. AI can analyse vast amounts of information—demographics, psychographics, online behaviour, market trends—to uncover hidden patterns and predict where your message will resonate most strongly.

Think about this, though: AI can't just generate content; it needs a human to provide the context. This is a critical point for using AI in content creation. It can help us streamline the process, generate ideas, and create engaging content, but it's still up to us to provide the context and direction. AI is a tool, not a replacement for our creativity and expertise.

> Dan Martell has a great way of putting it in episode 45 of the *Amplify AI* podcast: AI is a content creator, not a context creator. In other words, you need to be able to define the problem, the goal, the vision, and the strategy. Then AI can help you generate the content to bring those ideas to life.

Here's how you can leverage AI to unlock new markets:

Identify Lookalike Audiences

AI can analyse your existing customer data to create a detailed profile of your ideal customer. Think of it as creating an avatar—understanding their demographics, interests, behaviours, pain points, and aspirations. Then, AI can scour the digital landscape to identify 'lookalike audiences'— groups of people who share similar characteristics with your existing high-value customers.

This allows you to target your marketing efforts with laser precision, reaching those most likely to convert. It's like having a matchmaking service for your business, connecting you with the perfect prospects.

Analyse Emerging Trends

AI can be your trend-spotter, monitoring online conversations, social media activity, search patterns, and even industry publications to identify emerging topics and interests that align with your brand.

This gives you a heads-up on what's captivating the attention of your potential customers, allowing you to adjust your content strategy and messaging to stay ahead of the curve. You'll have a finger on the pulse of the market, enabling you to anticipate shifts in demand and position your brand for maximum impact.

Uncover Untapped Geographic Markets

Your ideal customers might be clustered in locations you haven't even considered. AI can analyse geographic data, economic indicators, and cultural trends to reveal regions where your product or service is likely to find a receptive audience.

This takes the guesswork out of expansion, enabling you to prioritise markets with the highest potential for success.

It's like having a global market research team working for you 24/7, uncovering hidden gems of opportunity around the world.

Explore New Platforms and Channels

The digital landscape is constantly evolving, with new platforms and channels emerging all the time. AI can track the rise of these platforms and analyse user demographics and behaviours to determine which ones hold the greatest potential for reaching your target audience.

This ensures your marketing efforts are focused on the channels where your message will have the most impact, maximising your reach and return on investment.

Test and Iterate

Prediction is an ongoing process. AI can analyse the performance of your marketing campaigns and provide insights on what's working and what's not. This allows you to continuously refine your targeting, messaging, and channel strategies, ensuring you're always maximising your reach and impact in new markets.

The power of AI to predict new markets is transformative. It empowers you to:

- **Reduce Risk**: Instead of blindly entering new markets, you can make data-driven decisions, minimising wasted resources and increasing your chances of success.

- **Maximise Growth**: By identifying high-potential markets, you can accelerate your growth trajectory and expand your brand's reach and impact.

- **Unlock New Opportunities**: AI can reveal possibilities you might never have seen on your own, opening doors to new customer segments, geographic regions, and even innovative business models.

As you navigate the exciting world of AI-powered market prediction, remember:

1 **Data Quality Matters**: The accuracy of AI's predictions depends on the quality and comprehensiveness of the data you feed it. Ensure your data is clean, accurate, and representative of your target audience.

2 **Human Intuition Still Counts**: While AI can provide invaluable insights, don't discount the power of human intuition and experience. Use AI as a strategic partner to augment your own judgement, not replace it.

Predicting new markets is a process of discovery, a chance to take your brand to places you never imagined possible. Embrace the power of AI, stay agile, and always be ready to explore the uncharted territories of opportunity that await.

Amplify Impact

Building an audience is one thing. Creating a movement is another. Amplifying your impact goes beyond reaching more people; you want to make a difference in their lives. It's about igniting a spark that inspires action, drives positive change, and leaves a lasting legacy. And in the age of AI, we have unprecedented tools at our disposal to do just that.

But AI alone isn't the answer. True impact comes from a genuine connection with your audience, from understanding their needs, their aspirations, and the challenges they face. It comes from building trust, fostering a sense of community, and consistently delivering value that resonates on a deep, human level.

I believe that when we talk about using AI ethically and for good, we need to consider our values and purpose. We cannot focus on technology without understanding the deeper meaning behind our work.

My friend Shafaat Hashmi, a successful entrepreneur and investor, believes that spirituality is the fuel for our purpose. He says that spirituality gives us a foundation for our value system, a sense of humanity, and a deeper understanding of our role in the world. Shafaat also emphasises that the purpose is not static. It evolves as we grow and learn. We need to constantly re-evaluate our goals and aspirations, and adapt to the changing world around us.

> Find Shafaat Hashmi speaking about this on the *Amplify AI* podcast. For myself, I think my personal values include developing and empowering people and understanding the humanity behind business. I cover this idea of the integration between spirituality and business in episode 57.

Here's how to use AI to amplify your impact and create a movement that matters.

Embrace the Power of Storytelling
Stories have the power to move hearts and minds. They create emotional connections, inspire action, and make your message unforgettable. AI can be your storytelling partner, helping you craft compelling narratives that resonate with your audience. Use AI to:

- **Uncover Hidden Stories**: Analyse customer data and feedback to identify powerful stories of transformation, success, and overcoming challenges.

- **Personalise Your Narratives**: Tailor your stories to resonate with different audience segments, creating a deeper sense of connection.

- **Scale Your Storytelling**: Repurpose your stories across multiple channels, from social media to email to blog posts, maximising their reach and impact.

It's time to turn data into narratives that resonate. Let AI be your partner in crafting stories that move hearts, inspire action, and amplify your message like never before.

Build a Community of Shared Purpose

A loyal audience isn't just a group of followers; it's a community of people united by shared values, goals, and a desire to make a difference. AI can help you cultivate this sense of community by:

- **Connecting Like-Minded Individuals**: Use AI to facilitate interactions between your audience members, creating opportunities for collaboration, support, and shared learning.

- **Personalising the Experience**: Tailor communications and recommendations to each individual, fostering a sense of belonging and making them feel valued.

- **Amplifying Collective Voices**: Use AI to curate and share user-generated content, showcasing the diversity and impact of your community.

With AI as your ally, you can cultivate a community that's more than just a list of names on a spreadsheet. Create a tribe of passionate advocates who are ready to join you on your mission and make a real difference together.

Become a Catalyst for Positive Change

True impact extends beyond your business. True leaders contribute to something bigger than themselves, tackle meaningful challenges, and create a better world. AI can empower you to be a catalyst for positive change by:

- **Identifying Opportunities for Impact**: Analyse data and trends to uncover areas where your business can make a real difference.

- **Scaling Your Efforts**: Use AI to automate and optimise your impact initiatives, maximising your reach and efficiency.

- **Measuring Your Results**: Track the impact of your efforts and use data-driven insights to continuously improve your approach.

It's time to step up, embrace our role as changemakers, and use the tools at our disposal to create a future we can all be proud of.

Champion Authenticity and Transparency

In a world saturated with noise and superficiality, authenticity and transparency are more important than ever. Use AI to:

- **Share Your Journey**: Be open and honest about your successes, challenges, and lessons learned, building trust and relatability.

- **Give Back to Your Community**: Use AI to identify meaningful ways to support causes that align with your values.

- **Promote Ethical AI Practices**: Be transparent about how you use AI and advocate for responsible development and deployment.

In the AI age, authenticity is your superpower. Let your values guide you, be transparent in your actions, and show your audience the real people behind the brand. That's how you build trust, loyalty, and a movement that stands the test of time.

Empower Your Audience to Take Action

Impact isn't a passive pursuit; it requires action. Empower your audience to become active participants in your movement by:

- **Providing Clear Calls to Action**: Make it easy for your audience to get involved, whether it's donating to a cause, sharing your message, or taking steps to improve their own lives.

- **Equipping Them with Tools and Resources**: Use AI to create educational content, guides, and resources that help your audience achieve their goals and make a difference.

- **Celebrating Their Contributions**: Recognise and acknowledge the efforts of your audience, fostering a sense of shared accomplishment and momentum.

Give your audience the tools, inspiration and roadmap to make a difference. Together, we can amplify our collective impact and create a ripple effect that transforms the world, one action at a time.

Incorporating AI into your strategy for audience growth leads to transformation. With the Amplify AI Pyramid as your guide, you can grow an engaged and loyal audience that will ensure your brand's success in the digital era. Remember, the power is in your hands to use AI not just to grow your numbers, but to grow your impact and create a *movement that matters*.

I've compiled a list of prompts that you can use to grow your audience using the steps here. Find them at: amplifyais.com.

CHAPTER 11

GROW OPERATIONS

*Imagine having a super-powered
assistant that can sift through data, spot
patterns, and suggest improvements faster
than any human could. That's AI.*

W HAT IF THE way you run your business today is
already becoming obsolete? The truth is, the pace
of technological advancement, especially with AI, is
accelerating exponentially. To operate and innovate
in this new time, we must understand the forces shaping the
future of work and embrace the transformative power of AI.
This chapter explores three key timelines and the concept of
commoditisation to help future-proof your operations and
build a legacy of operational excellence.

Understanding our evolution through the three timelines
of the *Industrial*, *Information*, and *Intelligence* Revolutions
means understanding the chapters of humanity's ongoing
narrative. Each revolution has escalated our capabilities,
from mechanisation to digitisation to what we have today:
intelligence augmentation and cognitive enhancement.

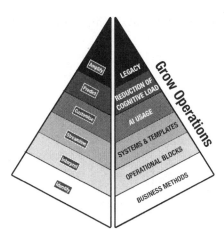

Commoditisation is a critical piece of this puzzle. Each revolution commoditised industry, information, and intelligence respectively. This commoditisation suggests that what was once a unique advantage—be it steam power, computing capabilities, or AI—eventually becomes accessible to all, levelling the playing field. For a business, this means that leveraging AI is not an option but a necessity to stay in business. This underlines the importance of integrating AI in a way that complements your company's unique strengths.

The ChatGPT Earthquake: Intelligence Becomes a Commodity

Each revolution commoditised something once exclusive. First, it was industry, with machines replacing muscle. Then information, with computers turning data into readily available insights. Now, we're in the thick of the Intelligence Age, and guess what's becoming a commodity? You got it—intelligence itself.

I remember when ChatGPT hit the scene in late 2022. It felt like a seismic shift, a bit like that first 'aha!' moment when I truly grasped the power of the internet. Suddenly, everyone was buzzing about AI, and for good reason. This wasn't just a shiny new toy; it was a new way of thinking, creating, and interacting with information.

It had an immediate impact on my work. I started using ChatGPT to brainstorm podcast episode ideas, generate show notes, even write compelling marketing copy. And I wrote my own AI software called WriteFlow[13] using OpenAI and ChatGPT's API. Creating WriteFlow[13] AI has allowed me to tick a huge goal off my list—to write and sell useful software myself.

You can find more about my AI software at amplifyais.com/writeflow.

I had just arrived into Cebu on a Saturday morning on an Emirates flight from Dubai. I had the weekend to play with AI. So I started thinking, what would my constraints be?

* Can I create something we can use immediately?

* I don't want to create a new platform. Can I use something people are already used to?

* Could I create something useful and needed now?

* Can I use intelligence to achieve outcomes at speed?

By the end of Sunday, I had a working copy of WriteFlow[13], which does everything from a SWOT analysis to content writing and more. What used to take hours was now done in minutes, freeing up my mental bandwidth to focus on strategy and the bigger picture.

And it wasn't just me. Businesses across all industries started experimenting with this new form of accessible intelligence. Remember the printing press? Before Gutenberg, knowledge was a luxury, hoarded by the elite. The printing press democratised information, leading to a surge in literacy and the spread of ideas. AI is doing something similar today. My friend and business expert Dale Beaumont often uses a powerful analogy to explain the impact of AI on industries. Think of a photo from early 20th century New York City. Horse-drawn carriages clog the streets, with a single automobile struggling to find its place. Fast forward a decade, and the picture is reversed—cars are everywhere, and the horse-drawn carriage is a relic of the past. AI is at that tipping point now. What was once slow is about to become very, very fast. Industries that don't adapt will be left behind, like that lone carriage in a sea of automobiles. Your core business might be safe for now, but the way you operate every department will be disrupted.

> Tune into episode 68 of the *Amplify AI* podcast to hear my chat with Dale.

But let's pause for a second. Just like we saw with the printing press and e-readers, this sudden accessibility of AI is raising some serious ethical questions. With the printing press, we saw the rise of propaganda and the spread of misinformation. With e-readers, we saw concerns about copyright infringement and the demise of traditional bookstores. Now, with AI, we're grappling with the potential for bias in algorithms, the erosion of privacy, and even the displacement of jobs.

We must be mindful of these potential downsides. We can't just rush into AI adoption without considering the consequences. We have a responsibility to use this technology for good, to amplify our humanity, without creating divisions or inequalities.

What can we learn from the past? The printing press and e-readers ultimately led to positive changes, but not without some bumps along the way. We have to use AI ethically and responsibly. It's not all about what AI can do; it's about how we, as humans, choose to use it.

Just like e-readers disrupted the publishing industry, changing how we read and consume content, AI is poised to revolutionise the way we work, create, and do business. It's empowering people to do things they never could before—generate creative content, analyse data, automate tasks, and even write code.

Take marketing, for example. Instead of sending generic messages, you can now use AI to tailor content and offers to each individual's interests and behaviours. That's game-changing!

> Find my interview with Curtis Schmidt on episode 71 of the *Amplify AI* podcast). He talks about how AI-powered tools are now making it possible to personalise campaigns with laser precision.

And customer service? Think AI chatbots, those tireless virtual assistants who are now handling routine enquiries, freeing up human agents to tackle complex issues that require empathy and creativity.

Even education and healthcare are being transformed. AI is personalising learning experiences, providing customised feedback, and grading assignments. In healthcare, AI is assisting with diagnosis, predicting patient outcomes, and driving the development of life-saving new drugs.

The implications for business operations are immense. The companies that embrace AI and adapt their processes will thrive. Those that cling to outdated methods and resist change risk being left behind, like that lone horse-drawn carriage in a sea of automobiles.

AI Won't Take Your Job, but People Using AI Will

You'll hear it all the time: 'AI is going to take all our jobs!' But that's not necessarily true. Think about it—if you're still washing clothes by hand for three hours, you're probably not using your time wisely. Don't fear AI; embrace it and use it to your advantage. AI isn't going to replace jobs; it's going to make people who don't use AI look inefficient. And let's be honest, that's going to make a difference in today's competitive landscape.

The truth is, AI is more likely to take on the role of co-pilot, a powerful tool that helps us work smarter and more efficiently.

> My friend Dan Martell, a tech entrepreneur and investor, has been saying this for years, and he's right. Listen to him on the *Amplify AI* podcast in episode 45.

We've seen how the Industrial Age commoditised industry and the Information Age commoditised information. Now we're in the Intelligence Age, where intelligence is becoming a commodity. AI is making it easier to process information, automate tasks, and generate creative content.

AI is a catalyst for reimagining what's possible. It can help us solve problems we couldn't even imagine before. Think about Instagram—it wouldn't have been possible without the innovation of the iPhone.

Today, AI is providing us with new opportunities to create, innovate, and make a difference. Don't be afraid to play with it and experiment. You might be surprised what you discover.

It's time to head into the final quadrant of the Amplify AI Pyramid's six-step process to grow operations. Let's achieve the goals of the business while keeping the focus on brand identity and good ethics.

Identify Business Methods

Every business, regardless of size or industry, has a process for delivering its service or product to customers. Your processes create the backbone of your operations and dictate how resources (like time, budget, and staff) are used. Understanding and documenting these internal processes isn't simply boring paperwork; it's the starting line for identifying where AI can supercharge your efficiency.

Consider an online marketing consultant. She has a four-step process taking clients from 'overwhelmed' to 'confident in my marketing': (1) Strategy Planning Session, (2) Content Creation, (3) Distribution and Engagement, and (4) Review and Iteration. Each step has substages and defined client deliverables.

By taking stock and clearly articulating her method, this consultant highlights where AI can help: streamlining her content creation using text and image generators, or automating portions of her social media distribution using intelligent social media management tools.

If you don't have it down, now is where you document your method. I'll give you another example. If a company hires me to help them adopt AI in their business, I will give them the six-step Amplify AI Pyramid and its four quadrants. I'll ask them what they would like to focus on and what they want to grow. Then I'll follow the process documented in this book.

If you are a business that wants to use a podcast to grow revenue, credibility, and audience, then I'll direct you towards the AMPLIFY framework from my first book so you can do it piece by piece.

How to implement this step:

1. Map out your core process(es), showing how you deliver the result your client wants.

2. Use flowcharts or checklists to make this visual.

3. Ask: Are there bottlenecks or friction points in this process?

4. Consider which sub-tasks might be candidates for AI support.

1. Documentation Is Key

Begin by mapping out your core process(es), showing how you deliver the result your client wants. This documentation should be as detailed as possible, covering not just the main stages but also the subtleties and nuances of each interaction. This could range from the initial consultation to the final feedback loop. The goal here is to have a crystal-clear blueprint of your method that leaves no stone unturned.

2. Visualise the Process

Once documented, translate this information into a visual format, like a flowchart or process map. Visual representations can unveil inefficiencies, redundancies, or opportunities for enhancement that text alone may not reveal. They enable you to step back and see the entire client journey from a bird's-eye view, making it easier to pinpoint where AI can play a transformative role.

3. Identify Bottlenecks and Friction Points

With your process visually laid out, identify areas where bottlenecks occur or where clients experience friction. These are the points where clients could feel frustration or where your resources are disproportionately drained. Highlighting these areas provides a focused lens through which you can consider AI solutions. For instance, if scheduling consultations is a bottleneck, an AI-driven scheduling tool could provide a more streamlined, efficient solution.

4. Pinpoint Opportunities for AI Integration

Now, scrutinise each step for tasks that are repetitive, require significant manual input, or could benefit from predictive insights. These are prime candidates for AI integration. For example, if content creation is a core part of your method, AI-powered content generation tools could drastically reduce the time and effort involved, freeing up your creative resources for higher-level strategic thinking.

Throughout this process, refer to the SymbioEthical Framework for a structured approach to ethically integrating AI into your operations. This serves as a strategic framework, guiding you from identifying your business method through to leading the market with innovative AI applications. By aligning your AI initiatives with the ethical parameters, you ensure that every technological enhancement is ethically and purposefully directed towards amplifying your business's core strengths and value proposition.

Identifying and refining your business method with AI starts as an exercise in enhancing operational efficiency, but becomes a transformative experience that redefines how you deliver value to your clients. By meticulously mapping out your business method and strategically integrating AI, you unlock new levels of agility, precision, and personalisation in your service delivery. This sets you apart in a competitive market and deepens the trust and loyalty of your clients, ensuring your business grows and sets the example in the digital age.

We're not implementing AI for the sake of innovation here. The ultimate goal is to fundamentally enhance the core of what your business promises and delivers. In doing so, you set a new standard for excellence in your industry, paving the way for a future where AI and human ingenuity combine to create unparalleled value.

Interpret Operational Blocks

Remember Charles Darwin's famous quote: 'It is not the strongest of the species that survives, nor the most intelligent that survives. It is the one that is most adaptable to change.' This is truer than ever in the age of AI. Clinging to outdated skills or resisting change is a recipe for obsolescence. Those who thrive will be the ones who embrace flexibility, seek out new knowledge, and constantly adapt to the evolving demands of the marketplace.

Interpreting operational blocks is about diagnosing the health of your business's core processes. Just as a doctor uses symptoms to identify underlying issues, businesses can use data and AI to uncover and address inefficiencies within their operations. This section goes into how businesses can leverage AI to diagnose and rectify operational blocks, ensuring a smooth and efficient cycle from awareness to delivery.

Businesses generally revolve around three core phases:

1 **Awareness**: Attracting attention from potential customers.

2 **Conversion**: Transforming leads into paying clients.

3 **Delivery**: Fulfilling your promise, keeping clients satisfied, and generating testimonials.

Each of these stages plays a critical role in the business cycle, from attracting potential customers to transforming leads into satisfied clients who are eager to share their positive experiences. However, just like any process, this cycle can encounter blocks—obstacles that impede smooth operation and optimal performance.

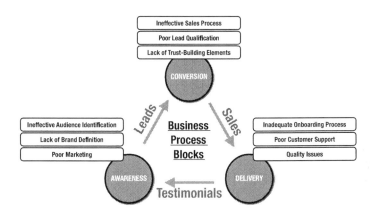

Your first hurdle is diagnosing where, precisely, help is needed within this cycle. AI tools, coupled with insightful analytics, empower you to pinpoint the roadblocks to smooth operations. This also offers a precision that goes beyond gut feelings or surface-level assessments.

If a software company finds a consistent delay in user onboarding, this is an operational block that could be flagged using insights from customer support ticket data. AI can be introduced to analyse historical data to help pinpoint patterns and potential causes of this delay. It can even point to solutions—such as refining help documentation using natural language processing (NLP) tools, or pre-emptively targeting certain demographics with automated onboarding tutorials. Let's look at how to implement this step.

1. Analyse Data Across Phases

The first step in diagnosing operational blocks is to conduct a thorough analysis of data from various segments of your business. This involves collecting and scrutinising data from customer feedback, sales cycle lengths, and support ticket logs, among other sources. The objective of this data collection is to synthesise this information to paint a clear picture of your operational health. Here are some ideas to start with:

Customer Feedback: The Mirror of Your Performance

Start by reviewing the feedback your customers provide. This is the mirror reflecting your business's external image. Are there recurring complaints or suggestions? This feedback can often highlight issues in your Delivery phase or even earlier in the Awareness or Conversion phases.

Sales Cycle Length: The Timeframe Indicator

Next, examine the length of your sales cycle. Is it longer than industry standards or your own expectations? Extended sales cycles might indicate blocks in Conversion, suggesting that potential clients are getting lost or losing interest along the way.

Support Tickets: The Direct Line to Problems

Finally, analyse your support ticket data. A high volume of tickets or consistent issues can signal operational inefficiencies, particularly in the Delivery phase. Are there common themes or specific stages where clients seem to struggle?

2. Look for Patterns

With the data, the next step is to identify patterns. This is where AI truly shines. AI tools, with their capability to process vast amounts of data rapidly, can detect recurring issues that might elude human analysis. These patterns serve as indicators of where your operational cycle is stumbling.

For example, if there's a noticeable trend in customer feedback about delayed responses during the Conversion phase, AI can help pinpoint this as a critical area for improvement. Similarly, patterns in sales cycle data might reveal specific stages where prospects consistently drop off, signalling the need for a strategic intervention.

3. Identify Blind Spots

Every business has blind spots—areas that may seem efficient on the surface but that, upon closer inspection, harbour inefficiencies. AI's prowess in data analysis can help unveil these hidden areas. For instance, a pattern of delayed project kick-offs post-sale may not be immediately obvious without analysing the specific timelines and feedback associated with these instances.

By leveraging AI for deep data analysis, you can uncover these inefficiencies. Whether it's an overlooked step in the onboarding process or a bottleneck in customer support, identifying these blind spots is the first step towards rectification.

4. Focus on Critical Pain Points

Once you've identified patterns and blind spots, the temptation might be to overhaul everything. However, the key to effective improvement lies in setting priorities. Choose one significant pain point to address first. This should be an issue that impacts your operations significantly and has proved resistant to previous attempts at resolution.

Prioritising for Impact

Focusing on the most critical pain point allows you to channel your resources effectively. If data reveals that your Conversion phase suffers due to potential clients losing interest, this is where AI can make a significant impact. Implementing AI-driven CRM tools to personalise follow-ups or using AI to analyse potential client interactions for improvement opportunities can transform this phase.

Implementing AI Solutions

Once a critical pain point is identified, the next step is to explore AI solutions tailored to address it. For example, if the Delivery phase is your biggest challenge, with clients expressing dissatisfaction with the onboarding process, AI can offer solutions. Automated onboarding sequences, personalised through AI to match client profiles and needs, can significantly enhance client satisfaction and reduce operational blocks.

If attracting leads is your stumbling block, AI-powered market analysis tools can help you understand your audience better, enabling you to create more targeted marketing campaigns. If conversion is the issue, AI can enhance lead scoring and personalise communication, making it more likely that leads will turn into customers. And if delivery is where you're falling short, AI can streamline processes, automate tasks, and ensure that your promise to the customer is fulfilled more efficiently and effectively.

I found an article in the *International Journal of BIM and Engineering Science* about the inefficiencies of maintenance management systems within service buildings (more riveting than it sounds!). This 2024 study by Mais, Fayez, and Sanaa AL Mezawy (2024), showcases an interesting use of Building Information Modelling (BIM) and Business Intelligence (BI) to revolutionise how maintenance data is archived and analysed.[49]

By developing a BIM model for a university building and integrating five years of maintenance data for analysis, these researchers pinpointed prevalent maintenance issues and costs and forecasted future budgets and planned maintenance types.

Their findings show potential for a digital transformation in maintenance management across educational institutions, emphasising the strategic deployment of BIM and BI to enhance operational efficiency and predictive planning, and demonstrating a scalable model for optimising maintenance practices through data-driven insights.

The process of diagnosing operational blocks to implementing AI solutions should not be complex. The goal is to simplify: identify the most pressing issue, use AI to understand it deeply, and then apply a targeted solution. The goal of AI integration is not to use technology for the sake of it. It's to make strategic interventions that enhance your business's operational efficiency and effectiveness.

One of the biggest challenges for solopreneurs is transitioning into a team. One of the biggest hurdles is delegation. Rather than handing off tasks, you must understand how to give clear instructions and context to your team.

> In episode 62 of the *Amplify AI* podcast, Daniel Priestley talks about AI as your first employee. AI is really good at taking on those repetitive tasks, but it needs clear instructions and context to be effective. He says, 'AI is like a twenty-three-year-old who just graduated, but it doesn't know what to do.' It's our job as business owners to provide that guidance and context so that AI can be our most valuable team member.

Daniel also emphasises the importance of developing a strong team culture. Teams that leverage AI and embrace continuous learning are going to be the ones that thrive.

In episode 61, Daniel shares a great analogy: Think of a bakery where the baker spends a lot of time making sponge cakes. What if there were a machine that could create those sponge cakes automatically? That would free up the baker to focus on the creative tasks, like icing and decorating, that really make the cakes special. That's what AI can do for you. It can handle the heavy lifting, freeing you to focus on the human aspects of your work—the things that make you unique.

Streamline Business SOPs

Standard Operating Procedures (SOPs) outline your business's routine tasks and who is responsible for them. Ideally, SOPs make everything from client invoicing to new hire training clear-cut and predictable. Well-defined SOPs streamline processes and reduce the overall cognitive load on staff.

Use cases for AI are just exploding. There are thousands of new possibilities.

A lot of businesses today are working with outdated information and making decisions based on gut feel. AI allows us to get real-time insights, reduce human error, and free up our brains for more creative and strategic thinking.

> In episode 18 of the *Amplify AI* podcast, Jere Simpson discusses how AI can help businesses become more efficient and effective. He compares using AI to using Waze or Google Maps. If those tools were always twenty minutes behind, they wouldn't be very useful.

Streamlining your business's SOPs gives your operations a well-deserved upgrade. It means every cog in your machine turns smoothly, efficiently, and purposefully. When your SOPs are on point, they're like a trusty roadmap guiding your team through their tasks, ensuring consistency and quality at every turn.

At We Are Podcast, we call our SOPs our Regular Recurring Reps or RRRs. These tasks, from daily client communication to monthly invoicing, keep our business steadily achieving its goals. They ensure we're always in tune with our goals and our audience's needs.

But SOPs aren't meant to be static. They must evolve with your business. As you grow, your processes must adapt.

Imagine having a super-powered assistant that can sift through data, spot patterns, and suggest improvements faster than any human could. That's AI. It's like having a brilliant strategist on your team, working 24/7 to streamline your operations.

Let's paint a picture. Say you're a business with onboarding documents scattered across folders and emails. It's a nightmare for new hires to navigate, eating up valuable time better spent on meaningful work.

Enter AI. With the right tools, AI can scan all these documents, no matter where they're hiding. It can consolidate, organise, and even flag inconsistencies or outdated information. Suddenly, your onboarding process goes from a scavenger hunt to smooth sailing.

But this goes beyond organisation. AI can also help identify processes ripe for streamlining. It can analyse workflows, pinpoint bottlenecks, and suggest improvements. Maybe it notices a task taking twice as long as it should or spots a redundant step in your process. AI brings these insights to light, giving you the power to optimise your operations like never before.

Now, implementing AI might sound daunting, but it doesn't have to be. Start strategic and small. Here's how:

1 **Audit your SOPS.** Dive deep into your current processes. Are they up to date and easily accessible by your team? This audit gives you a clear picture of where you stand and where you need to go.

2 **Standardise your SOPS.** Ensure all your SOPS follow a specific template. Consistency makes it easier for your team to follow and reference them, and for AI to analyse and improve them.

3 **Harness AI tools.** Some AI-powered tools can 'read' your SOPS, spot inconsistencies, and suggest improvements. They're like a keen-eyed editor, ensuring your SOPS are always polished and effective.

4 **Identify processes needing streamlining.** Use AI to identify these opportunities. Maybe it's automating part of your invoicing or streamlining client onboarding. Every improvement, however small, adds up.

5 **Remember the human touch.** While AI works wonders, it doesn't replace human judgement. Use AI to free up your team's time and cognitive load, but always keep the

human element at the heart of your operations. Let AI handle repetitive tasks so your team can focus on innovating, creating, and building meaningful client relationships.

Streamlining your SOPs with AI empowers your team to do their best work. When your processes are smooth and optimised, your team can focus on what really matters— delivering incredible results for your clients and driving your business forward.

At We Are Podcast, streamlined SOPs have freed up our team's time and mental energy. We've focused on creating engaging content, building deep relationships with our audience, and pushing the boundaries of podcasting.

And that's the real goal, isn't it? Use technology to create space for innovation and growth. When you streamline your SOPs with AI, you're doing more than optimising your operations. You're setting your business up for a future where your team thrives, your clients succeed, and your impact is truly amplified. Pun intended.

Head to amplifyais.com to find a template checklist for regularly streamlining SOPs using AI, along with recommended Generative AI prompts and assumptions.

Customise AI Usage

Customising AI doesn't mean using every fancy tool. It means finding the right solution that integrates seamlessly with your existing workflow and offers demonstrable results. It requires an 'experiment and analyse' mindset, one that stays focused on solving those core operation bottlenecks you identified. Not only do you need to find the right tools; you need to use them effectively.

> In episode 45 of the *Amplify AI* podcast, Dan Martell talks about how his team created 'DanGPT', a custom AI model trained on his own knowledge base. This allows his team to quickly answer questions, generate content, and even find relevant resources for coaching clients. That's the power of AI—it can be customised to meet your specific needs. It's about thinking beyond the box and creating a system that works for you.

Imagine the online marketing consultant from our earlier example. She identified her content creation stage as an area ripe for AI assistance. To customise the solution, she may do the following:

1 **Define Needs**: Does she struggle with image generation for social media? With writing persuasive marketing copy? Is it more time-consuming for her to generate ideas or polish rough drafts? Being specific is key.

2 **Research Relevant Tools**: There's an overwhelming ocean of AI tools. Start with reputable platforms like OpenAI (ChatGPT, DALL-E) or popular industry-specific options. Look for AI tools designed to solve the specific challenge identified.

3 **Implement, Test, and Adapt**: Begin by applying the tool with a small test project. Evaluate how outputs integrate into the consultant's existing content creation workflow, and what time/effort is saved. Tweak AI prompts and fine-tune workflows, iterating over time for better outcomes.

When it comes to customising AI usage for your business operations, it's crucial to focus on tailoring solutions that address your specific needs and goals. Off-the-shelf AI tools can provide a starting point, but true operational transformation comes from adapting AI to fit your unique business processes like a glove.

This is where techniques like handling missing data, feature selection, and hyperparameter tuning come into play.[50] By carefully curating your datasets, identifying the most predictive features, and finetuning your AI models, you can develop solutions that are laser-focused on enhancing your operations. It's about leveraging AI not as a one-size-fits-all tool, but as a precision instrument crafted to optimise your business's unique operational rhythm.

Imagine AI as a skilled tailor, carefully measuring and adjusting algorithms to create a bespoke suit that fits your business perfectly. By investing in this customisation process—cleaning data, selecting key variables, tweaking model settings—you ensure that AI augments your operations in the most impactful way possible. The result is an AI strategy that feels custom-made for your business, amplifying efficiency and performance in a way that aligns seamlessly with your processes and goals.

Remember that customisation is key. Embrace the process of adapting AI to your business's unique contours, and you'll unlock its true potential as a catalyst for operational excellence. There is not one AI solution that works for everyone—you need to create one that works perfectly for you.

How to implement this step:

1   Don't reinvent the wheel—leverage industry recommendations.

2   Start with free (trial) versions whenever possible.

3   Consider scalability: Will the tool become redundant as you grow?

4   Remember, AI doesn't replace human thinking; it augments it.

Predict the Reduction of Cognitive Load

It's one thing to say AI makes things 'easier', but how do you truly quantify its impact on your team's workload and overall wellbeing? Cognitive load refers to the mental effort required to process information and complete tasks. High cognitive load leads to employee stress, burnout, and, ultimately, inefficiencies. AI, strategically implemented, can greatly reduce this load. Here's how you can approach this...

Let's imagine a customer service team drowning in a daily flood of support tickets. An AI-powered tool is introduced to categorise customer enquiries. Tickets tagged as basic FAQ issues get auto-resolved. Now, staff primarily handle complex questions requiring higher analytical skills. Over time, they may observe reductions in:

1 **Employee Stress**: Measured by feedback surveys or reduced sick days.

2 **Response Times**: Analytics see improved responsiveness due to the reduced mental load of not having to sort through easy-answer queries.

3 **Team Turnover**: A less burdensome workload enhances job satisfaction.

How to implement this step:

1 Focus on quantifying the load reduction, with more than anecdotal evidence.

2 Look for 'before/after' AI implementation performance metrics.

3 Remember, employee morale is directly linked to cognitive load.

4 Assess how much freeing up bandwidth opens opportunities for innovation within your team.

Amplify Legacy

Your legacy as a leader isn't tied solely to revenue or industry disruption. True impact occurs when operational excellence meets ethical stewardship, benefiting employees and clients alike. AI offers tools to amplify a legacy built on core values. Let's see how to frame this impact.

Imagine a CEO who commits to AI that aligns with the value of 'Customer Care'. Leveraging customer data to analyse feedback for product improvement is seen as aligned with the value. However, AI only reinforces legacy when its use complements what the brand stands for, so this means using AI for lead generation is scrapped if it relies on intrusive data-gathering that violates user privacy.

AI can be a powerful tool for improving employee wellbeing. By automating repetitive tasks and streamlining workflows, you can reduce cognitive overload and free up your team to focus on more meaningful, creative work. A happy, engaged team is a productive team, and that's a legacy you can be proud of.

How to implement this step:

1   Refer to your 'Symbiotic Framework' to guide decision making here.

2   Explain AI adoption choices to both teams and clients.

3   Legacy-enhancing use cases could include using AI for:

a   Improved accessibility features for disabled clients.

b   Optimised internal training to create higher skilled staff.

c   Reduced environmental impact of business operations.

4   Highlight and share these use cases with your industry.

The true power of AI lies not in its ability to automate or optimise, but in its potential to amplify our humanity. Let's use AI to bridge divides, not widen them. Let's use it to solve meaningful problems collaboratively, not hoard solutions for ourselves. Let's use it to build a more equitable, sustainable world for everyone, not just a select few.

> As my friend Kylie Ryan so eloquently put it in episode 83 of the *Amplify AI* podcast, 'What can we see in each other that is the same that we can align on?' That could be a guiding principle in adopting AI.

Remember the days when only a small percentage of houses had electricity? It felt like something out of a science fiction movie. Well, that's where we are with AI right now. It's a vital resource that everyone should have access to, not just the select few. And just as it became an ethical imperative to make electricity accessible to all, the same applies to AI. We need to ensure that AI is used for good, to amplify human potential, not to create divisions or inequalities.

I've compiled a list of prompts that you can use to grow operations using the steps here. Find them at: amplifyais.com

CONCLUSION
OUR NEXT STEPS

YOU HAVE ACCESS to the #1 ranked graduate on the planet. For $20 a month or less, you can access the graduate at the top of their class. Valedictorian not just in one field, but in Business, Medicine, Law, Marketing, Strategy, Engineering, and much more. This is AI.

What are you going to ask it to do? Are you going to learn to use it ethically, to achieve your business goals?

We know AI is learning from us. AI is learning from our data. And the data captured so far has majorly highlighted the idea that for someone to win, others have to lose. And that if you are the most intelligent species, it makes you the most powerful. And that it is okay to go after money and wealth without thinking of the destruction left in our wake. If that is what the data is saying, then that is what AI will learn. That is why we need to capture more stories of collaboration and love and a change in our consciousness.

The world is changing. I've always found it weird that a human is born and has to be trained for at least ten years in schools to operate on the planet. And then educated for another six years or more to be 'useful' on the planet. What if the future is there for us to learn to be good humans instead of learning new skills? Imagine going to school to learn humility, collaboration, listening, and being of service.

I wonder if, with Artificial Intelligence, we can become focused more on human being than human doing. Remember, intelligence is a commodity. You are not.

We've covered a lot of ground in this journey, haven't we? From demystifying AI to building ethical frameworks to crafting a roadmap for business transformation. But if there's one thing I want you to take away, it's this: AI is a force for good. It's a powerful ally, yes, and it's an ally that can amplify our humanity, not replace it.

The key is integration, but not *just* integration—*ethical* integration. It's about weaving AI into the fabric of our businesses in a way that aligns with our values, respects our customers, and makes a positive impact on the world.

We need to recognise that our actions have ripple effects, that we're all interconnected, and that our responsibility extends beyond ourselves. And that brings us to the big picture—the triad of intelligence. A symphony where Human Intelligence, Artificial Intelligence, and Divine Intelligence all play their part, creating something far greater than the sum of their parts.

How can we bring this symphony of intelligence to life in our businesses?

The 3 Ways to Implement the Frameworks in This Book

Three is a magic number. Just as a triangle—and each face of a pyramid—has three sides, there are three ways of implementing what you've learned in this book.

1. Values First

When using this approach you are starting with the question, 'How can I augment my human intelligence with Artificial Intelligence and align it with divine intelligence?'

First, identify core values, ethical principles, and ethical AI frameworks. Understanding the SymbioEthical Framework, you embrace the values most important to you. You define what 'divine intelligence' means in the context of your goals and principles. This may involve principles like compassion, empathy, sustainability, global collaboration, and ethical responsibility. Aligning AI with these values ensures that technological advancements contribute positively to humanity and the planet, reflecting a higher wisdom or 'divine' aspect. You then create or adopt ethical guidelines for AI development and use. This involves ensuring AI respects privacy, promotes fairness, and is transparent and accountable. By embedding ethical considerations into AI, you ensure that the technology serves humanity's best interests, aligning with the notion of 'divine intelligence' upholding ethical and moral standards.

You augment intelligence through the Amplify AI Pyramid using AI tools and platforms to enhance cognitive functions, such as decision making, creativity, and problem solving. Examples include AI for data analysis, predictive modelling, and natural language processing. These tools can help humans process information more efficiently and make more-informed decisions, effectively augmenting human intelligence with the speed and scale of AI.

Throughout, you integrate ancient wisdom, continuous learning, and collaborative AI development with modern technology. You combine insights from ancient wisdom traditions with AI technologies. For instance, applying principles from mindfulness and ethics in AI algorithms or interfaces. This integration ensures that AI applications are technically advanced and enriched with the depth of human wisdom, reflecting a balanced approach between technology and spirituality.

You foster global collaboration in AI development, involving diverse stakeholders to ensure the technology is inclusive and benefits all of humanity. Collaboration ensures a multiplicity of perspectives, aligning AI development with a more holistic and 'divine' intelligence that values unity and diversity.

You establish mechanisms for continuous feedback and learning, allowing AI systems to adapt over time in alignment with ethical standards and human values. This ensures AI systems remain relevant and beneficial, reflecting an ongoing commitment to growth and improvement, similar to a 'divine' journey towards wisdom.

2. Quadrant First

In this approach, depending on where you are in your business as a leader and the current needs of your business, you can pick which quadrant of the pyramid you want to focus on. Do you want to grow revenue, brand, audience, or operations?

If you need profit, focus on growing revenue first. Then, I would focus on growing the brand and amplifying trust next. This way you have credibility in your marketplace and when you start focusing on growing your audience, the audience you attract will stay longer.

If your business already has good profit, credible trust in the market, and a steady flow of new audience, then focus on growing operations.

3. Step First

This is a layered approach to AI adoption using the Amplify AI Pyramid. Start with identifying business goals, brand identity, business vision, and business methods. Next, based on what you've identified in Step 1, you interpret the business vital signs, brand guidelines, audience WHY stack, and business operational blocks. Next streamline, then customise, before predicting and amplifying.

I recommend this method only to organisations that already have good profits through the revenue coming in. These businesses need to have brand trust in their marketplace, continuously create impact with their audience, and have an established legacy through elevated operations. If you are a business that is already thriving and you want to adopt and integrate Artificial Intelligence in a holistic manner, then this is the way to go.

The Code

When it comes to next steps, some of you may want to execute them straight away. Now that you know the framework and understand the rules, you can either follow or break the rules as you head into customising and personalising the Amplify AI Pyramid for you and your business.

If you've gotten to this point in your reading, then you are ready for the Code. The Code is your fuel booster, enabling you to implement this whole framework at speed. I have built this whole framework into an AI assistant that can execute this for you and your business.

Go to amplifyais.com and find 'The Code'.

Did I Explain Why Using AI Ethically Is Imperative?

Look, I get it. All this talk about ethics might feel a bit 'touchy feely' when you're trying to run a business, hit those targets, and stay ahead of the curve. But here's the thing: Ethics aren't just some abstract concept; they're the bedrock of trust. And in today's world, trust is the most valuable currency you can have.

Think about it. Would you trust a business that's using your data without your knowledge or consent? Would you trust an AI system that's making decisions based on biased data? Would you trust a company that's prioritising profit over the wellbeing of its employees, its customers, or the planet?

I sure wouldn't. And neither would your audience.

That's why using AI ethically isn't just the 'right thing to do'; it's the smart thing to do. It's about building a business that people can believe in, a brand that stands for something more than just the bottom line.

Throughout this book, we've talked about the potential pitfalls of AI—bias, privacy violations, even job displacement. But we've also explored the incredible opportunities—solving meaningful problems, amplifying human potential, and creating a more equitable and sustainable world.

The choice is ours. We can either use AI to build a brighter future, or we can let it lead us down a path of division and distrust.

I know which path I'm choosing. What about you?

The Biggest Conversation of Our Lifetime—and Using Your Voice

When I think about the impact of AI, I always think back to my podcast conversation with Jere Simpson. Jere shared a powerful analogy: think of AI as a thousand tongues in your pocket. It's like having a superpower that gives you instant access to information.

> Check out episode 18 of the *Amplify AI* podcast to listen to my chat with Jere.

Jere also emphasised the importance of starting relationships with AI in the right way—a symbiotic way. We need to see AI not as a slave or a competitor, but as a powerful ally.

AI is going to continue to evolve, but it's up to us to determine how we use this incredible tool. Let's use AI to create a better world, one that's more equitable, more sustainable, and more filled with human connection and empathy. Let's make AI work for us, not against us.

This, my friends, is easily the biggest conversation of our lifetime. It's time to have your say.

REFERENCES

1   Lynch, S. (2023). 2023 State of AI in 14 Charts. [online] Stanford HAI.
    Available at: https://hai.stanford.edu/news/2023-state-ai-14-charts.

2   Oxford insights (2023). Gov AI Readiness Index. [online] Oxford
    Insights. Available at: https://oxfordinsights.com/ai-readiness/
    ai-readiness-index/.

3   Oluwatoyin Ajoke Farayola, Adekunle Abiola Abdul, Blessing Otohan
    Irabor, & Evelyn Chinedu Okeleke. (2023). INNOVATIVE BUSINESS
    MODELS DRIVEN BY AI TECHNOLOGIES: A REVIEW. Computer
    Science & IT Research Journal, 4(2), 85-110.

4   O'leary, lizzie (2022). How IBM's Watson Went from the Future of
    Health Care to Sold Off for Parts. Slate. [online] 31 Jan. Available at:
    https://slate.com/technology/2022/01/ibm-watson-health-failure-
    artificial-intelligence.html.

5   Strickland, E. (2019). How IBM Watson Overpromised
    and Underdelivered on AI Health Care. [online] IEEE
    Spectrum. Available at: https://spectrum.ieee.org/
    how-ibm-watson-overpromised-and-underdelivered-on-ai-health-care.

6   NVIDIA. (n.d.). NVIDIA Deep Learning Technical Resources. [online]
    Available at: https://www.nvidia.com/en-au/training/resources/
    [Accessed 4 Apr. 2024].

7   Applied Software, GRAITEC Group. (2023). 6 Ways Prodsmart
    Can Help Optimize Manufacturing Production. [online] Available
    at: https://asti.com/blog/6-ways-prodsmart-can-help-optimize-
    manufacturing-production/ [Accessed 4 Apr. 2024].

8   Unity. (n.d.). Unity AI—Create Incredible Experiences with Real-Time
    3D. [online] Available at: https://unity.com/ai.

9   Affectiva. (2017). Home—Affectiva. [online] Available at: https://www.
    affectiva.com/.

10 www.sensetime.com. (n.d.). SenseFoundry—Digital City Operation—
    SenseTime. [online] Available at: https://www.sensetime.com/en/
    product-business?categoryId=1077&gioNav=1.

11 Losey, R. (2017). Future of Life Institute 2017 Asilomar Conference.
    [online] AI Ethics. Available at: https://ai-ethics.com/2017/08/11/
    future-of-life-institute-2017-asilomar-conference/ [Accessed 4 Jan.
    2024].

12 A-COA: an adaptive cuckoo optimization algorithm for continuous and combinatorial optimization H.R. Boveiri and M. Elhoseny, December 2018 Neural Computing and Applications 32(3).

13 Amplify AI. (n.d.). WriteFlow AI—Write Faster and Better | AI-Powered Tool. [online] Available at: https://amplifyais.com/writeflow.

14 Verma, Jyotsna & Kesswani, Nishtha. (2015). A Review on Bio-Inspired Migration Optimization Techniques. International Journal of Business Data Communications and Networking. 11. 24-35. 10.4018/IJBDCN.2015010103.

15 Duman, Ekrem & Uysal, Mitat & Alkaya, Ali. (2011). Migrating Birds Optimization: A New Metaheuristic Approach and Its Application to the Quadratic Assignment Problem. Information Sciences. 217. 254-263. 10.100⁷⁄₉₇₈-3-642-20525-5_26.

16 Wikipedia Contributors (2024). Lotka–Volterra equations. [online] Wikipedia. Available at: https://en.wikipedia.org/wiki/Lotka%E2%80%93Volterra_equations#Dynamics_of_the_system.

17 Jorge Guardiola, Fernando García-Quero, Buen Vivir (living well) in Ecuador: Community and environmental satisfaction without household material prosperity?, Ecological Economics, Volume 107, 2014, Pages 177-184, ISSN 0921-8009, https://doi.org/10.1016/j.ecolecon.2014.07.032. (https://www.sciencedirect.com/science/article/pii/S0921800914002456).

18 Te Pa Tu (2022). 3 Māori Concepts That Will Change the Way You See the World. [online] Tamaki Māori Village. Available at: https://te-pa-tu.com/our-stories/3-maori-concepts-that-will-change-the-way-you-see-the-world/.

19 The First Nations Information Governance Centre. (n.d.). Home. [online] Available at: https://fnigc.ca/.

20 Anon, (2019). Pikialasorsuaq Commission | Inuit Circumpolar Council Canada. [online] Available at: https://www.inuitcircumpolar.com/icc-activities/pikialasorsuaq-commission/ [Accessed 14 Jan. 2024].

21 ogimaamikana.tumblr.com. (n.d.). Ogimaa Mikana: Reclaiming/Renaming. [online] Available at: https://ogimaamikana.tumblr.com/.

22 Hawkins, D. (2014). Power vs. Force: the Hidden Determinants of Human Behavior: Author's Official Authoritative Edition. Hay House Inc.

23 Morandín-Ahuerma, Fabio. (2023). IEEE: a global standard as an ethical AI initiative.

24 Sado, F., Loo, C., Kerzel, M., & Wermter, S. (2020). Explainable Goal-Driven Agents and Robots—A Comprehensive Review and New Framework. ArXiv.

25 Becks and Weis (2022).

26 Lepri, B., Oliver, N., & Pentland, A. (2021). Ethical machines: The human-centric use of artificial intelligence. iScience, 24. https://doi.org/10.1016/j.isci.2021.102249.

27 Ntoutsi, E., Fafalios, P., Gadiraju, U., Iosifidis, V., Nejdl, W., Vidal, M., Ruggieri, S., Turini, F., Papadopoulos, S., Krasanakis, E., Kompatsiaris,

I., Kinder Kurlanda, K., Wagner, C., Karimi, F., Fernandez, M., Alani, H., Berendt, B., Kruegel, T., Heinze, C. and Broelemann, K. (2020). Bias in Data driven Artificial Intelligence systems—An Introductory Survey. WIRES Data Mining and Knowledge Discovery, [online] 10(3). doi:https://doi.org/10.1002/widm.1356.

28 Mahmud, B., Hong, G., & Fong, B. (2022). A Study of Human–AI Symbiosis for Creative Work: Recent Developments and Future Directions in Deep Learning. ACM Transactions on Multimedia Computing, Communications and Applications, 20, 1-21. https://doi.org/10.1145/3542698.

29 Fu, Frank & Yi, Hong & Zhai, Nanji. (2013). Training to Improve New Product Sales Performance: The Case of Samsung in China. Performance Improvement. 52. 10.1002/pfi.21346.

30 Magaletti, Nicola and Cosoli, Gabriele and Leogrande, Angelo and Massaro, Alessandro, Process Engineering and AI Sales Prediction: The Case Study of an Italian Small Textile Company (February 4, 2022).

31 Alnakhli, Hayam & Inyang, Eddie & Itani, Omar. (2021). The Role of Salespeople in Value Co-Creation and Its Impact on Sales Performance. Journal of Business-to-Business Marketing. 28. 347-367. 10.108%1051712X.2021.2012079.

32 Lemon, K. N., & Verhoef, P. C. (2016). Understanding Customer Experience Throughout the Customer Journey. Journal of Marketing, 80(6), 69-96. https://doi.org/10.1509/jm.15.0420.

33 Guenzi, P., De Luca, L.M. and Spiro, R. (2016), The combined effect of customer perceptions about a salesperson's adaptive selling and selling orientation on customer trust in the salesperson: a contingency perspective, Journal of Business & Industrial Marketing, Vol. 31 No. 4, pp. 553-564. https://doi.org/10.1108/JBIM-02-2015-0037

34 Wang, J., Ioannis Ivrissimtzis, Li, Z. and Shi, L. (2024). Enhancing User Experience in Chinese Initial Text Conversations with Personalised AI-Powered Assistant. doi:https://doi.org/10.1145/3613905.3651104.

35 Lemon, K.N. and Verhoef, P.C. (2016). Understanding Customer Experience Throughout the Customer Journey. Journal of Marketing, [online] 80(6), pp.69–96. doi:https://doi.org/10.1509/jm.15.0420.

36 Kienzler, Mario & Kindström, Daniel & Brashear, Thomas. (2018). Value-based selling: a multi-component exploration. Journal of Business & Industrial Marketing. 34. 10.1108/JBIM-02-2017-0037.

37 Zhang, C., Tian, Y.-X. and Fan, Z.-P. (2021). Forecasting sales using online review and search engine data: A method based on PCA–DSFOA–BPNN. International Journal of Forecasting. doi:https://doi.org/10.1016/j.ijforecast.2021.07.010.

38 Namaki, M.S.S.E. (2019). How Companies are Applying AI to the Business Strategy Formulation. Scholedge International Journal of Business Policy & Governance ISSN 2394-3351, [online] 5(8), p.77. doi:https://doi.org/10.19085/journal.sijbpg050801.

39 Huang, J.Y., Gupta, A. & Youn, M. Survey of EU ethical guidelines for commercial AI: case studies in financial services. AI Ethics 1, 569–577 (2021).

40 The art of pricing in the age of AI. (2023). Available at: https://
assets.ey.com/content/dam/ey-sites/ey-com/en_in/topics/
consulting/202³⁄₀₉/ey-the-art-of-pricing-in-the-age-of-ai.pdf.

41 Grand View Research (2022). Artificial Intelligence Market Size,
Share | AI Industry Report, 2025. [online] Grand View Research.
Available at: https://www.grandviewresearch.com/industry-analysis/
artificial-intelligence-ai-market.

42 Chen, B., Wu, Z. and Zhao, R. (2023). From fiction to fact: the growing
role of generative AI in business and finance. Journal of Chinese
Economic and Business Studies, 21(4), pp.1–26. doi:https://doi.
org/10.1080/14765284.2023.2245279.

43 Link to external site, this link will open in a new window (2023).
Chinese Brand Identity Management Based on Never-Ending
Learning and Knowledge Graphs. ProQuest, [online] p.1625.
doi:https://doi.org/10.3390/electronics12071625.

44 Dhruba Charan Bihari (2023). Artistic Influences in Business
Organisations to Establish a Brand. *Paripex Indian Journal of Research*,
pp.38–40. doi:https://doi.org/10.36106/paripex/1003957.

45 Yanqin, W. and Kaiju, C. (2020). Decoding the Mystery Behind the
Globalization of Chinese Time-honored Brands—A Case Analysis of
Lao Gan Ma Chili Sauce. International Journal of Literature and Arts,
8(2), p.87. doi:https://doi.org/10.11648/j.ijla.20200802.18.

46 SA Jawaid and J Qureshi (2024). How Artificial Intelligence and
Machine Learning Can Impact Market Design.

47 Hamid, I., Anwar Ramli, Muhammad, Tenri Sayu Puspitaningsih
Dipoatmodjo and Ruma, Z. (2022). The Effect of Social Media
Marketing on Sales (Case Study of WASHYOURSHOES in Makassar
City). International Journal of Humanities, Social Sciences and
Business, 1(3), pp.353–359. doi:https://doi.org/10.54443/injoss.v1i3.36.

48 Al Naqbi, H., Bahroun, Z. and Ahmed, V. (2024). Enhancing
Work Productivity through Generative Artificial Intelligence: A
Comprehensive Literature Review. Sustainability, [online] 16(3),
p.1166. doi:https://doi.org/10.3390/su16031166.

49 Mais, Fayez and Sanaa AL Mezawy (2024). Developing a Model to
Improve the Efficiency of Maintenance Management for Service
Buildings Using BIM and Power BI: A Case Study. 8(1), pp.18–30.
doi:https://doi.org/10.54216/ijbes.080102.

50 Zita, C. (2022). 5 Effective Ways to Improve the Accuracy of Your
Machine Learning Models. [online] Medium. Available at: https://
towardsdatascience.com/5-effective-ways-to-improve-the-accuracy-
of-your-machine-learning-models-f1ea1f2b5d65.

51 Vaz, R. (2017). The perfect recipe for a deep conversation.
[online] www.ted.com. Available at: https://www.ted.com/talks/
ronsley_vaz_the_perfect_recipe_for_a_deep_conversation.

APPENDIX
PODCAST EPISODE LIST

ALL PODCAST EPISODES can be found at amplifyais.com/ podcast or search for *Amplify AI* on YouTube, Spotify, or wherever you get your podcasts. Here is a list of all episodes referenced in this book.

EPISODE NO.	CHAPTER	EPISODE DESCRIPTION
#18	Conclusion	How to plug your business data into AI to make better business decisions feat. Jere Simpson
#30	10	Driving business growth with AI: the scoreapp. com feat. Glen Carlson
#36	5	Nature's Algorithms and AI, featuring ornithologist Jean-Phillippe Schepens Van Thiel
#45	10, 11	AI as a tool for streamlining business processes, featuring entrepreneur Dan Martell
#48	6	Discussing the power of AI with entrepreneur Gary Vaynerchuk
#54	10	The illusion of skill in AI, featuring entrepreneur Leopold Ajami
#57	10	The integration of spirituality and business in the age of AI, featuring entrepreneur and investor Shafaat Hashmi

ACKNOWLEDGEMENTS

EFORE WE wrap up this wild ride, I want to take a moment to thank the people who made it all possible. It's only fair that I give them the recognition they deserve!

First and foremost, my rock-solid wife, Rochelle—without you, I'd be lost (literally!). Your unwavering support means the world to me. You can be a pain sometimes, but it usually means I can have a spiritual awakening later. You let me be myself.

Mum and Dad, your guidance and wisdom have shaped me into the person I am today. Thanks for investing so much in me and giving me such a great childhood!

To my incredible team—I couldn't have done it without each and every one of you! Special thank you to Venz Ricardo. Sara, my editor, helped me shape this book into something I'm truly proud of. Not just this one, she was instrumental in my first book too.

A special thank you to Scott MacMillan and the Grammar Factory Publishing team. I loved working with you.

And to my ancestors, thank you for paving the way—your stories and your sacrifices inspire me.

Now, let's get to some amazing people and institutions who've made an impact on my life:

- Liverpool FC—what can I say? You're more than just a football club; you're a symbol of hope and perseverance.

I love everything you embody as an institution. Best reality TV series ever... You'll never walk alone!

- My teachers—you are the unsung heroes! Your patience, expertise, and encouragement (sometimes lack of) helped me become the person I am today. Thanks for being there when I was ready to learn!

- My mentors—I've been blessed to have had some incredible guides along the way. Thank you for sharing your wisdom and experience with me!

- The Key Person of Influence program—the guidance and mentorship of this program meant everything to me during a pivotal time in my life.

- My family—thank you for the grounding and belief. Especially to Bubbles and Renson, Papa, Mama, my aunts and uncles, cousins, and my extended MMT, BlackBelt and KPI families. I love that you will have me in your lives.

To all my podcast guests, thanks for being willing to share your stories and expertise with me! And to my clients—you've trusted me with your problems, and I'm honoured to have been able to help.

Special shout-outs to Taki and Kiri-Maree Moore (I learn so much from everything you both do), James Orsini, Chris Dufey (WriteFlow wouldn't have been a thing if not for you), Kylie Ryan (each session with you helped me grow), Daniel Priestley, Mike Reid, and Glen Carlson (KPI was the best for me), Amy Yamada, Gary Vaynerchuk, Ken Droz, Darin Olien, Rod Santomassimo—you all make my life richer just by being in it!

I have learnt leadership, how to take a loss, and how to do the right thing from Jürgen Norbert Klopp (yeah, that's him!). Boss, I'm so glad you are a Red.

And last but certainly not least... I wanna thank myself!

Without all the work, study, and writing this wouldn't have happened. It's a reminder that we're always learning, adapting, and becoming better versions of ourselves. I thank all amazing versions of myself: past, present, and future. Your evolution has been cool to watch.

That's it! To everyone who's played a part in making this book possible—thank you for your love, support, expertise, and enthusiasm.

This book is for the artist. For the dreamer. For the authentic leader.

This book is for all of us!

ABOUT
THE AUTHOR

HEY THERE, I'm Ronsley, and I'm on a mission to help you raise your voice and change the world. As a life-long tech geek, entrepreneur, and storyteller, I've spent the last decade using my voice to inspire, educate, and empower folks like you to amplify your message and make a real difference.

I've been pulling computers apart since I was twelve and broke my first phone at two by plugging it into an electric socket (sorry, Mum!). That curiosity led me to a Bachelor's in Computer Science and Engineering, a Master's in Software Engineering, and, finally, an MBA focused on Psychology and Leadership. Because here's the thing—understanding people is just as important as understanding code.

But my real passion? Helping people share their stories. That's why I dived headfirst into the world of podcasting twelve years ago. Since then, I've created top-rated shows like *Amplify AI*, *We Are Podcast*, *Bond Appetit*, and *The Psychology of Entrepreneurship*, reaching over 5.1 million listeners across 133 countries. I even had the honour of giving a TEDX Talk on the power of deep conversations, which was made a TED Talk (check it out on TED.com!).[51]

Through my podcast agency, We Are Podcast, I've helped over 1,200 businesses and individuals raise their voices and help their businesses stand out in a crowded market by using a podcast. We've worked with everyone from entertainers and athletes to government leaders, politicians, and entrepreneurs, crafting podcasts that engage, inspire, and drive real business results.

But as the digital landscape shifted, I saw the first part of my career (computer science) and the second part (entrepreneurship and podcasting) merging—bringing in the AI revolution. This was about more than automating tasks; it was about unlocking human potential on an entirely new level. That's why I programmed Writeflow AI[13] and founded Amplify AI, a training and advisory company that helps businesses adopt AI ethically and effectively. We're not just chasing the latest tech trends; we're building a future where AI empowers people to achieve the extraordinary.

Of course, it's not all work and no play. When I'm not geeking out over AI or podcasting, you might find me rock climbing on a new continent (four down, three to go!), whipping up a gourmet meal (did I mention I'm a qualified chef and had my own restaurant?), or swapping stories with deep thinkers about how to make the world a little bit better.

No matter what I'm doing, my core belief remains the same: there has never been a better time to use your voice, speak your truth, and make sure the right people hear you. Especially if you have a business you believe in.

That's why I wrote AMPLIFY and why I'm so excited to share *Amplify AI* with you.

Whether you're a solopreneur, a small business owner, or the CEO of a large enterprise, *Amplify AI* provides the tools and knowledge you need to navigate the AI revolution. Embrace this opportunity to create a legacy of positive impact and innovation.

Join the movement towards a smarter, ethical future. Let *Amplify AI* be your guide.

See you on the inside!

Made in the USA
Coppell, TX
16 November 2024